What "They" Say .

All ministry leaders need to cultivate healthy and life-giving friendships, with peers and especially with Jesus. Unfortunately the concept of friendship has been reduced to clicks and "likes" on social media sites that are neither life-giving nor truly signs of friendship. Hank Voss, using the wisdom of Aelred of Rievaulx, reorients us to the great value and depth of true and lasting friendships and to their centrality in generous and holistic service to others.

~ Rev. Greg Peters, PhD,
Professor of Medieval and Spiritual Theology,
Torrey Honors College, Biola University

As a pupil of Bernard of Clairvaux and his *Sermons on the Song of Songs*, Aelred focused on being God's friend (John 14:1). Aelred's *Spiritual Friendship* is an excellent book, both of scholarship and of devotion.

~ James M. Houston, DPhil,
Professor Emeritus of Spiritual Theology,
Regent College

In an age of information overload, globalization, increasing isolation, and individualism, we need the reminder that friendships among Christians can be holy and life-giving, and indeed provide the needed accountability for faithful, fruitful, long-term ministry. From my own experience as a single in ministry, life can be lonely . . . but it does not have to be. Thanks to Aelred and Hank Voss, we have that reminder.

~ Stephanie Lowry, PhD,
Lecturer in Theology and Programme Coordinator,
Africa International University

Spiritual Friendship: Learning to Be Friends with God and One Another

© 2022. The Urban Ministry Institute. All Rights Reserved.

ISBN: 978-1-955424-06-6

Published jointly in 2022 by TUMI Press and Samuel Morris Publications.

TUMI Press is a division of World Impact, Inc.

TUMI Press
The Urban Ministry Institute
3701 E. 13th Street, Suite 100
Wichita, KS 67208

Equipping Leaders. Empowering Movements.

Samuel Morris Publications:

Samuel Morris Publications
Sacred Roots Project at Taylor University
236 W. Reade Avenue
Upland, IN 46989

Samuel Morris Publications publishes texts in service to the evangelical church's life together and its ongoing pursuit of a deeper conformity to Jesus Christ (Galatians 4:19).

SACRED ROOTS SPIRITUAL CLASSICS

"Toward Ten Thousand Tozers"

Spiritual Friendship:
Learning to Be Friends with God and One Another

SACRED ROOTS SPIRITUAL CLASSICS 3

Edited by Rev. Dr. Hank Voss

Table of Contents

Acknowledgments

There are many to whom I owe thanks for this volume: to my parents who are now also friends; to my first friends and siblings—Isaac and Abigail, Brad and Kiki, David and Jamie, Jon, Matt and Corrie, Mark and Ashley, Tim and Lauren, Brandon and Mary, Aaron; to the many friends of my youth—especially Jon and Ben; to Klaus for both being a friend and for introducing me to the importance of friendship as a pathway to God; to my friends and fellow workers from World Impact—Susie, Ricardo, Heidi, Hector and Lucero, Jorge and Zully, Terry, Judson, Michelle, Tammy, Tracy, Grace, Tim, Don and Cathy, Bryan, Jenn and Rob, Fernando, Virgil, Todd, Bob and Susan, Bob and Chris, Scott and Gina, Marcos and Susie, Dave and Laura, Ryan and Danielle, Illiana and Jorge, Aaron and Lorraina, Byron, and many more; to the faculty and staff of The Urban Ministry Institute (especially Rev. Dr. Don Davis without whose encouragement this project would never have been launched. Don, thanks for being a "friend and fellow warrior"); to friends from Wheaton—especially Dan, Matthew, Carmen, Jay, and Stephanie; to my current colleagues at Taylor University—especially Mike, Phil, Kevin, and Jenny; to my former students, many of whom I can also call friends, especially to those who worked on this spiritual classic—Loyal Juraschek, Cheyenne King, Clay Wright, Nathan Peters, Jayden Wilhelm, Mary Hawthorne, Sam Wolowski and Gillian Haenggi; to all of these I say thank you.

I am especially thankful to Mark Williams, Professor Emeritus of Classics at Calvin College for permission to use his 1994 translation as the base for this Sacred Roots Spiritual Classic edition of *Spiritual Friendship*. I am also grateful to Dr. Jeff Gingerich, Provost at University of Scranton, for permission to use Williams' translation which was originally published by Scranton University Press. Thanks also to David Duncan for timely aid in sorting through various copyright issues related to this volume.

A special word of thanks is due to some additional people: to Father Francis Benedict, who introduced me to Aelred during a weekend retreat and has since remained an encouraging friend; to James Houston, whose pioneering work exploring the frontiers of friendship has led the way for this project, who kindly hosted me and some dozen others for lunch and a discussion about spiritual classics (in his ninety-seventh year!), and who provided an endorsement for this volume (from a hospital bed);[1] to Uche Anizor, Rukshawn Fernando, Jeremy Treat, May Young, and Denise Flanders, for patiently enduring long conversations about the nature of friendship in concrete contexts; to the Thursday Morning Men's Prayer Group at

---

1   For a testimony to the power of friendship in a Christian leader's life see James M. Houston, *Memoirs of a Joyous Exile and a Worldly Christian* (Eugene, OR: Cascade, 2019).

Urban Light Community Church, for modeling faithful friendships; to Greg Peters and Ryan Carter, for their wise editorial feedback and to the team of teams that make up the Sacred Roots project, especially those who are regularly in the trenches with me—Isaiah Swain, Eric Himelick, and Bob Engel among many others; to Dan Bowell, Ashley Chu, and the staff at Zondervan Library, for their ongoing help with accessing resources on Christian friendship; to Isaiah Swain in particular, without whom this volume may never have finally come to completion and who spent countless hours laboring on various research and editorial items; to Samuel, David, Renee, and Isaiah, for being willing to explore friendship between parent and emerging adults; and to my best friend and "delight of my eyes," Johanna, for your patience and for modeling a continuous pursuit of the face of God.

CHRISTIAN MINISTRY

Translation Notes

This edition of Aelred's *Spiritual Friendship* would not be possible without the English translation completed by Dr. Mark Williams, Professor Emeritus of Classics at Calvin College. Williams' translation includes helpful scholarly resources including extensive notes and several explanatory essays. I have not included Williams' footnotes, although this edition's notes often include information gleaned from Williams. Interested readers should consult Williams' original work.

> *Aelred of Rievaulx's Spiritual Friendship.* Translated by Mark F. Williams. Scranton, PA: University of Scranton Press, 2002.

Williams' translation was made from the critical Corpus Christianorum Continuatio Mediævalis (CCCM) Latin edition edited by C. H. Talbot and Anselm Hoste. This Sacred Roots Spiritual Classic edition of *Spiritual Friendship* also made extensive use of the CCCM text.

Aelred of Rievaulx, Saint. "De spiritali amicitia." In *Aelredi Rievallensis, Opera omnia*, edited by Anselm Hoste and C. H. Talbot, 279–352. CCCM. Turnholti: Brepols, 1971.

This edition occasionally replaces Williams' translation with (what I deem) an easier-to-read translation, always acknowledged with a footnote or an endnote. Other translations used to create this edition include translations made by Lawrence Braceland, M. Eugenia Laker, James Houston, and Jacques Dubois. See below for bibliographical information.

> *Aelred of Rievaulx: Spiritual Friendship*. Edited by Marsha L. Dutton. Translated by Lawrence C. Braceland. Collegeville, MN: Cistercian, 2010.
>
> *Aelred of Rievaulx. Spiritual Friendship: The Classic Text with a Spiritual Commentary by Dennis Billy, C.Ss.R.* Translated by M. Eugenia Laker. Notre Dame, IN: Ave Maria, 2008.
>
> *The Love of God and Spiritual Friendship*. Edited by James M. Houston. Abridged. Portland, OR: Multnomah, 1983.
>
> Aelred of Rievaulx, Saint. *L'amitié spirituelle*. Edited by Jacques Dubois. Bibliothèque de spiritualité médiévale. Paris: Éditions Charles Beyaent, 1948.

For the Sacred Roots edition, I have usually modified Williams' translation from "men" to "people" and from "he" to "one" when the Latin appears to be referring to people in general rather than males in particular. Aelred's location in a monastery means that male pronouns will be the norm, but readers should recognize that he was far ahead of many in his belief that men and women could be friends and that as friends they were also equals (1.57–60; 3.100).

Given that our target audience are congregational leaders serving among the poor with varying levels of literacy, I have simplified and standardized the translation of several key words used by Williams.

1. "Base" has been adapted to "shameful."

2. "Benevolence" has been adapted to "good will" as in one who is willing good for the other person.

3. "Charity" is the normal English translation of the Latin *caritate* (*caritate* is, for example, the word used for "love" in the Latin translation of 1 Corinthians 13).[1] Given the nuances of this word, Williams translates it over ten different ways in his English translation of *Spiritual Friendship*. In order to make it easier to follow Aelred's argument about love in relation to friendship, I have simplified the English words used to translate *caritate* and its variants to three: "affection," "love," and "Christian love."

4. "Carnal" and "fleshly" are both used by Williams to translate *carnalis* and *carnalibus*. I have adapted the text so that "fleshly" is used consistently.

Aelred quotes extensively from Scripture and other ancient sources. When Aelred quotes Scripture I have

---

1 Liz Carmichael, *Friendship: Interpreting Christian Love, a History of the Interpretation of "Agape" as Friendship-Love in the Western Christian Tradition* (London: T & T Clark, 2004).

used the ESV translation unless Aelred's point is clearer from the Vulgate. Scripture references are given in relation to the ESV's modern verse and chapter divisions. Parenthetical references to citations and many allusions to Scripture have been added. Passages alluded to have their parenthetical references in italics, whereas passages with direct quotations are cited in regular font.

When quotations are from the Apocrypha, I have usually replaced the translation made by Williams with the NRSV; occasionally, I retained Williams' English translation of the Vulgate. Direct quotations from Cicero use either the 1913 Harvard Classics translation or Williams' translation depending on which I thought most clear.[2] Quotations from Ambrose occasionally are adapted to follow the translation of Davidson if I thought this would be helpful for readers.[3]

In quotations, I have usually updated the language to reflect American, rather than British, spellings (e.g. "honorable," not "honourable").

---

2   Cicero's text, *On Friendship*, is available in the public domain at the Internet History Sourcebook, www.sourcebooks.fordham.edu/ancient/cicero-friendship.asp.

3   Ambrose, *Introduction, Text and Translation*, vol. 1 of *Ambrose: De Officiis*, ed. Ivor J. Davidson, Oxford Early Christian Studies (New York: Oxford University Press, 2001).

Introduction

An Origin Story

"How important is friendship for the faithfulness, fruitfulness, and flourishing of serious disciples in the church today?" The first time I wrestled with this question was a cold January afternoon in 1995 when I was a freshman in college wandering around the Zondervan Library at Taylor University. I had a whole afternoon free with nothing to do and spent it walking up and down rows of books hoping to discover something interesting. I came across a series with more than thirty volumes and was amazed to discover it included books written by people who had studied with the Apostle John![1] Others had written their works within just a few generations of the last apostles, and all had been written during the first five centuries of the church.[2]

---

1   The series I discovered that day are called the Ante-Nicene Fathers (ANF) and the Nicene and Post-Nicene Fathers (NPNF). All of these books can be read for free at www.ccel.org/fathers.

2   You can read many of these early authors in Michael T. Cooper, ed., *Practices of the Ancient Church: Wisdom from the Apostolic Believers,* Sacred Roots Spiritual Classics 7 (Wichita, KS: TUMI Press, 2022).

I grew up in a wonderful church, but I had no idea these books still existed. Looking over them, I came across one written for pastors by an early church leader named Ambrose (d. 397). Ambrose mentored many younger church leaders, including an African pastor named Augustine (d. 430) who would become one of the most influential teachers in the history of the church. Later I would learn that Ambrose's book for pastors has been read and studied by those in spiritual leadership for more than sixteen hundred years; generations have found it helpful for understanding pastoral work.

At the time I stumbled across Ambrose's book, however, I had no idea of its importance, but I was curious. What caught my attention was the final chapter—a chapter on friendship. I still remember my surprise. "Why would somebody spend a whole chapter on friendship in a book for young pastors? And if you were going to spend a whole chapter on friendship, why would you put it as the final chapter in your book—as if encouraging pastors to invest in friendship was so important that you wanted this emphasis to be the final word in your book?" I had no idea why Ambrose included this chapter in his book, but it did raise the question:

> "Is friendship really vitally important for those called to spiritual leadership within the church?"

It took twenty years before I could explore the question more seriously. During that time I worked as a teacher, a church planter, a missionary, and a professor at The Urban Ministry Institute. I experienced the joys of friendship, the camaraderie of working with amazing women and men on the front lines of urban ministry. Many of these heroes of the faith have not just become friends for life, they have become "eternal friends"—we will be friends for eternity (1.22–24, 68; 3.134). I could write about my delight in these friends for many pages—truly their friendship has been one of God's greatest gifts to me.

But my experience with friends in ministry was not all positive. I also experienced painful betrayals of trust, the kind David writes about in Psalm 55:12–14.

> If an enemy were insulting me, I could endure it;
> if a foe were rising against me, I could hide.
> But it is you, a man like myself, my companion,
> my close friend, with whom I once enjoyed
> sweet fellowship at the house of God,
> as we walked about among the worshipers. (NIV)

All this to say, two decades of ministry led me to a preliminary answer to the question Ambrose's book had raised many years earlier. "Yes! Friendship is vitally important for spiritual leaders if we want to not just survive, but thrive, and to serve faithfully and fruitfully for a lifetime." The growing assurance I had about this answer is what led me in 2017 to sign up for a three-day retreat advertised with the title "Spiritual Friendship." I did not know much about the spiritual classic that would serve as the basis for the retreat, but I had heard of it before. Some years prior, my friend, Rev. Bob Engel had loaned me a book called *The Love of God and Spiritual Friendship*.[3] This book had selections from two friends who had lived in the twelfth century, Bernard of Clairvaux and Aelred of Rievaulx, and it was edited by a professor

---

3   Bernard of Clairvaux and Aelred of Rievaulx, *The Love of God and Spiritual Friendship*, ed. James M. Houston, Classics of Faith and Devotion (Portland, OR: Multnomah, 1983; reprint Vancouver, BC: Regent College, 2018).

at Regent College named James Houston—a man who had once been friends with C. S. Lewis.

Three good friends (Johanna, Uche, and Mel) and I spent a weekend learning about spiritual friendship from Aelred's *Spiritual Friendship*. Our teacher was Father Francis, a man who had lived with a dedicated group of disciples as a Benedictine monk for over fifty years. The retreat confirmed in my heart that there was deep wisdom in Aelred's little book for contemporary Christian leaders. When the opportunity came up to participate in the Sacred Roots Spiritual Classics series, I knew an edition of *Spiritual Friendship* would be my contribution.

Who Was Aelred of Rievaulx?

Aelred was born in AD 1110 to a family who had served in various positions of church leadership for generations. As a young man he was a steward to King David I of Scotland, but soon decided to leave court life and become a monk. In 1134, Aelred left Scotland and joined a new Cistercian monastery at Rievaulx, near Yorkshire in England.[4] He rose through various positions of leadership, and eventually became leader of the community, responsible for shepherding its many members. Aelred was an excellent leader, and the community grew from around three hundred to some six hundred and fifty during his tenure as abbot. One of Aelred's spiritual friends, Walter, (one of the three spiritual friends featured in *Spiritual Friendship*) wrote Aelred's biography.[5]

---

4 Aelred's community followed a rule of life developed by Saint Benedict around AD 600. For more information on what Aelred's daily life looked like see Greg Peters, ed., *Becoming a Community of Disciples: Guidelines from Abbot Benedict and Bishop Basil*, Sacred Roots Spiritual Classics 2 (Wichita, KS: TUMI Press, 2021).

5 Walter Daniel, *The Life of Aelred of Rievaulx: And the Letter to Maurice*, trans. Frederick Maurice Powicke, Cistercian Fathers 57 (Kalamazoo, MI: Cistercian, 1994).

Aelred was also a good friend of Bernard of Clairvaux, who was perhaps the most important Christian thinker of his century, and an expert on the topic of Christian love. Bernard urged Aelred to write, and so Aelred wrote a book about love called *The Mirror of Charity* as well as a number of other books. Aelred wrote *Spiritual Friendship* at the end of his life, sometime between 1164 and 1167, and it represents the fruit of decades of reflection on Christian community, Christian love, and spiritual friendship. Aelred saw Christian friendship as eternal (1.21). It offers a visible sign of Christ's kingdom come to earth.[6] Aelred believed that a spiritual friend is "the guardian of love—or, as some prefer to say, the 'guardian of the soul' itself" (1.20).

Sources for Spiritual Friendship

How did Aelred develop his understanding of spiritual friendship? What were his sources? Throughout history, Christian understandings of spiritual friendship at their best have sought wisdom from four sources.[7] First, Scripture, followed by three other areas: science (reason); the lived theology of the church (tradition); and experience. One reason Aelred's spiritual classic has remained helpful for over eight hundred years is that it draws wisely from all four of these sources. Aelred's example of exploring how Scripture, tradition, reason, and experience teach us about friendship is a model for disciples today.

---

6   Aelred of Rievaulx, *Spiritual Friendship: The Classic Text with a Spiritual Commentary*, ed. Dennis Billy, trans. M. Eugenia Laker (Notre Dame, IN: Ave Maria, 2008), 16.

7   See Uche Anizor, *How to Read Theology: Engaging Doctrine Critically and Charitably* (Grand Rapids: Baker Academic, 2018).

Table 1: Aelred's Wisdom on Spiritual Friendship Comes from Four Sources

Reason

Aelred learned from the wisest students of human relationships available to him. He collected insights from Cicero's study of human friendship called *On Friendship*.

Tradition

Aelred learned from many of the wisest teachers of the church who had come before him including leaders like Ambrose, Jerome, Augustine, Cassian, and Gregory the Great.

Experience

Aelred lived in a community of men who had all taken vows to pursue friendship with God and one another by following a discipleship plan known as *Benedict's Rule*. Within this community, Aelred was known as a legendary friend, and stories about his skill at friendship have been told for centuries.

Scripture

Aelred's life centered on Scripture. Like all members of his discipleship community, he spent a minimum of four hours a day, 365 days a year, reading, studying, meditating, and praying Scripture. He prayed through the book of Psalms every week, and lived in this rhythm for some four decades until his death on January 12, 1167.

As Table 1 indicates, the foundation of Aelred's understanding of friendship was Scripture. Aelred's spiritual classic engages extensively with Scripture, quoting or alluding to some thirty-four different biblical books. By apprenticing ourselves to Aelred, we learn to pay careful attention to the first human friendship described in the Bible—the friendship between Adam and Eve. Marital friendship is an important biblical theme that Aelred asks us to carefully consider, and he also draws our attention to friendships between Ruth and Boaz and between the married lovers in the Song of Solomon. Aelred also encourages us to consider the famous friendship between David and Jonathan, the friendship of Job and his companions, the friendships between Christ and his disciples, and the various friendships between members of the early church in Acts.

Second, Aelred considers wisdom on friendship gleaned from human reason's careful study of creation. For these insights into friendship from the natural world Aelred turns to a Roman writer named Cicero, who wrote a book called *On Friendship* (44 BC). Cicero collected wisdom from those who had carefully and intentionally studied human friendship in previous centuries (e.g. Plato and Aristotle). He summarizes this "creation wisdom" and put it into an interesting story in which two famous friends, Laelius and Scipio, talk about their personal friendship as an example of true friendship. Aelred listens carefully to Cicero's insights on friendship, but he brings those insights into service of his Christian worldview.[8]

If Aelred was writing today, in this subject area of "reason" he might also consider the Grant Study from Harvard Medical School. This study, begun in 1938, is one of the longest longitudinal studies of adult development ever done (over seventy-five years long). Its current director,

---

8   Marsha Dutton identifies some ninety-six citations or allusions to Cicero in Aelred's *Spiritual Friendship*. Aelred of Rievaulx, *Aelred of Rievaulx: Spiritual Friendship*, ed. Marsha L. Dutton, trans. Lawrence C. Braceland, Cistercian Fathers 5 (Collegeville, MN: Cistercian, 2010), 148. Where there are direct quotations, the Cicero reference is in the notes, and allusions are not always noted. See Dutton's text for additional discussion.

Robert Waldinger, claims that the study's clearest message is, "good relationships keep us happier and healthier. Period."[9] A similar message comes from *National Geographic's* Blue Zones project, which identified nine characteristics shared by happy, healthy, and long-lived peoples around the world. Friendship was one of these variables, and the researchers point readers to Japan where small groups of Japanese create *moais*, five friends who commit to each other for their entire life.[10] A third example comes from the research of Robin Dunbar who has spent a lifetime researching human friendship and social networks. He recently summarized the results from numerous studies—including one with over 300,000 participlants—and explained, "Perhaps the most surprising finding to emerge from the medical literature over the past two decades has been the evidence that the more friends we have, the less likely we are to fall prey to diseases, and the longer we will live."[11]

In addition to Scripture and reason, Aelred also gleans wisdom on spiritual friendship from the wisdom of the church (tradition). Aelred engages with wise Jewish and Christian leaders including ben Sira (c. 180–175 BC), Ambrose (d. 397), Jerome (d. 419) Augustine (d. 430), Cassian (d. 435), and Gregory the Great (d. 604). Every year for forty years (as required by the *Rule of St. Benedict*) Aelred would have read the spiritual classic *Conversations*, by Cassian (d. 435). In this spiritual classic Cassian

9   Robert Waldinger, "Transcript of 'What Makes a Good Life? Lessons from the Longest Study on Happiness,'" www.ted.com, November 2015.

10 Dan Buettner and Sam Skemp, "Blue Zones," American Journal of Lifestyle Medicine 10, no. 5 (July 7, 2016): 318–21.

11 Robin Dunbar, *Friends: Understanding the Power of Our Most Important Relationships* (Great Britain: Little, Brown, 2022), 7.

Cassian and Germanus Explore Spiritual Friendship as Friends

describes twenty-four conversations he and his good
friend Germanus had with various spiritual mentors. One
of the conversations was about friendship, and Aelred
alludes it some half dozen times (1.38, 46, 55; 2.53; 3.7,
37, 62). Marsha Dutton's edition of *Spiritual Friendship*
identifies well over one hundred allusions or citations from
these and other wise teachers of the church. The book for
pastors that I mentioned at the beginning of this introduction
(*On the Duties of the Clergy*), written by Ambrose, was a
favorite of Aelred's, and there are about forty allusions or
quotations to it in *Spiritual Friendship*.

Finally, Aelred did not simply study about Christian
friendship in Scripture, in creation (reason), and in church
teachings (tradition); he pursued and practiced spiritual
friendship in his own life (experience). Aelred believed in
community, and when he was a relatively young man he
was attracted to a Christian community with a high vision
of Christian friendship. This Cistercian community "by
the grace and love of the Holy Spirit" was "made 'of one
heart and of one soul.'"[12] In this community he invested
the next four decades of his life, and he became a beloved
mentor and friend. There is perhaps no better testimony
to Aelred's skill as a friend than his own dialogue with his
friends Ivo, Walter, and Gratian as described in *Spiritual
Friendship*. Even a man like Walter, who must have been
a very difficult person to get along with, was someone
Aelred was able to love and befriend.[13]

---

12 Walter Daniel, *The Life of Aelred of Rievaulx*, 98.

13 See for example how Aelred speaks to Walter in 2.1 and how he describes
immature friends in 3.17.

Structure of *Spiritual Friendship*

Spiritual Friendship was written as a book consisting of three conversations, each beginning with Aelred and a different friend. The first conversation (Book 1), takes place between Aelred and his friend Ivo. The second conversation (Book 2) takes place some years later and begins with Aelred's friend Walter, although a second friend, Gratian, soon joins them. The third conversation (Book 3) covers practical questions about spiritual friendship and includes Gratian and Walter again. This edition of *Spiritual Friendship* breaks the three books into eight chapters to help readers follow Aelred's argument and to align with the format of all Sacred Roots Spiritual Classics.

This edition also includes section headings within the chapters to help readers follow Aelred's argument about spiritual friendship. The section titles are original to this edition, although they are often based on insights from other editors like Jacques Dubois and Dennis Billy. Aelred himself provides good precedent for adding section headings. In his longer book, *Mirror of Charity*, he explains that he has added short section titles for his readers so that "the great length of this work may not frighten you, busy as you are."[14] He suggests readers look over the section titles "and having examined them, decide which you should read and which skip."[15]

Finally, the eight chapters also have paragraph numbers which start over at the beginning of each of the three

---

14 Aelred of Rievaulx, The Mirror of Charity, trans. Elizabeth Connor, Cistercian Fathers 17 (Kalamazoo, MI: Cistercian, 1990), 75.

15 Ibid.

conversations (Books). These paragraphs are standard and can be used when comparing this edition of *Spiritual Friendship* with others.

When citing Aelred we use the number of his conversation (Book 1, 2, or 3) and then the paragraph. For example, during his first conversation with Ivo about how long true friendship lasts, Aelred quotes Jerome (d. 420) in the 24th paragraph. We can reference this quotation as *Spiritual Friendship* 1.24, "1" refers to the first conversation (Book) and "24" to the paragraph. For reference, here is how Aelred's three conversations are divided in this edition of *Spiritual Friendship*.

Table 2: Structure of *Spiritual Friendship*

Sacred Roots Edition of *Spiritual Friendship*	Aelred's Divisions of *Spiritual Friendship*	Paragraph #s
Chapter 1	Prologue and Book 1: First Conversation, Part 1	1.1-30
Chapter 2	Book 1: First Conversation, Part 2	1.31-71
Chapter 3	Book 2: Second Conversation, Part 1	2.1-27
Chapter 4	Book 2: Second Conversation, Part 2	2.28-72
Chapter 5	Book 3: Third Conversation, Part 1	3.1-38
Chapter 6	Book 3: Third Conversation, Part 2	3.39-75
Chapter 7	Book 3: Third Conversation, Part 3	3.76-97
Chapter 8	Book 3: Third Conversation, Part 4	3.97-134

How Should I Read *Spiritual Friendship*?

For a variety of suggestions on how to read this spiritual classic with a group of friends see the appendix entitled "A Letter to God's Friends and Fellow Warriors on Why We Read the Sacred Roots Spiritual Classics Together." Specifically, for this volume you might consider reading the book over ten weeks (or ten meetings). If you do so, here is how I recommend dividing the reading.

Week	Section to Read before Meeting with Your Friends
Week 1	"A Letter to God's Friends and Fellow Warriors on Why We Read the Sacred Roots Spiritual Classics Together" (in Resources for Application) Introduction to *Spiritual Friendship*
Week 2	Chapter 1 and Discussion Questions
Week 3	Chapter 2 and Discussion Questions
Week 4	Chapter 3 and Discussion Questions
Week 5	Chapter 4 and Discussion Questions
Week 6	Chapter 5 and Discussion Questions
Week 7	Chapter 6 and Discussion Questions
Week 8	Chapter 7 and Discussion Questions
Week 9	Chapter 8 and Discussion Questions
Week 10	Afterword "Soul Work and Soul Care: Learning to Make Spiritual Friendship a Fine Art" (in Resources for Application)

Who Should Read *Spiritual Friendship*?

Who should read *Spiritual Friendship*? I suggest three groups of people who can especially benefit from this work: (1) spiritual leaders; (2) young people; and (3) married couples or single believers serious about Christian discipleship.

First, Aelred wrote this book for Christians who were serious about Christian discipleship and who were serving as spiritual leaders in their generation. In a similar way, I believe this book provides essential instruction for all who serve in positions of spiritual leadership today. If we hope to thrive in ministry, we must learn to practice the spiritual discipline of spiritual friendship.

Second, Aelred wrote this book to be an aide to the young. If you are a young person, then *Spiritual Friendship* was especially written for you. If you are trying to figure out how to construct a life that is beautiful, a life that shines the light and life and love of Jesus, then this book can help. Aelred's book provides a pathway to spiritual maturity that is marked by joy and happiness. If you take the time to read this book carefully, and to discuss it with good friends, you will discover a powerful spiritual discipline which will bring forth lasting fruit.

Finally, Christian married couples and Christian singles who want to flourish and provide a faithful witness to the goodness of Eden will find rich help in this book.[16] Aelred wanted all Christians to know God's creation design for the goodness and joy of human friendship. He wrote about

---

16 For a contemporary example of attending to married and single spiritual friendships see Peter Scazzero, *The Emotionally Healthy Leader* (Grand Rapids: Zondervan, 2015), 81–114.

spiritual friendship as a single man for other singles, but he clearly understood God's intention for every Christian marriage to also be an example of spiritual friendship.

Just as Aelred listened carefully to the wise teachers who came before him, our reading of Aelred can help us articulate what spiritual friendship might look like in our own generation. I pray that the same Holy Spirit, who taught our wise mentor and teacher Aelred about spiritual friendship, will also guide and teach you as you explore how to make faithful spiritual friendships in this generation.

Discussion Questions

 When do you remember making your first "friend"? What were the characteristics of that friendship?

 How important is friendship for all disciples of Jesus? What about those in spiritual leadership within the church? Which of the four subject areas revealing insight about friendship do you find most interesting (Scripture, tradition, reason, experience)? Why?

Have you ever thought of friendship as a spiritual discipline? Does recognizing that friendship with people on earth can help us grow in our friendship with God increase your desire to grow in the skill of making and keeping friends? Why or why not?

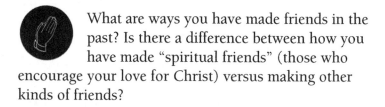 What are ways you have made friends in the past? Is there a difference between how you have made "spiritual friends" (those who encourage your love for Christ) versus making other kinds of friends?

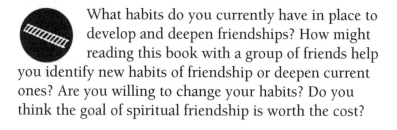 What habits do you currently have in place to develop and deepen friendships? How might reading this book with a group of friends help you identify new habits of friendship or deepen current ones? Are you willing to change your habits? Do you think the goal of spiritual friendship is worth the cost?

The Text

CHRISTIAN MINISTRY

Chapter 1

The Definition and Origin of Spiritual Friendship (Book 1.1–30)

For where two or three are gathered in my name, there am I among them.

~ Jesus, Matthew 18:20

Chapter Summary

Do you have a friend you could trust to guard your soul? Aelred's *Spiritual Friendship* provides encouragement that these kinds of friends can be found among Jesus' disciples. In this first conversation (Book 1) Aelred discusses spiritual friendship with his beloved friend Ivo, in the presence of their mutual friend, Jesus. Aelred and Ivo had been friends for a while, and Aelred had written a book several years earlier for Ivo, called *Jesus at the Age of Twelve*. Both this conversation in *Spiritual Friendship* and the earlier book

Aelred had written for Ivo illustrate how the two friends liked to use the eyes of their heart to imagine Jesus with them in the middle of everyday life.[1] Given their mutual love for Jesus, it is not surprising that their conversation about true friendship begins by picturing Jesus as a third conversation partner.

Aelred's conversation with Ivo is split between this chapter and the next. Aelred begins by introducing himself (Prologue) and his friend Ivo to establish the context and provide some background information (1.1-4). His style intentionally imitates Augustine's (d. 430) spiritual autobiography, Confessions. Aelred then explains why Christian friendship is better than the friendship described by the Roman writer Cicero (1.5-10). After Ivo asks Aelred for a definition of true spiritual friendship, they start with the definition Cicero provides in his classic book On Friendship (1.11-20). They then discuss how spiritual friendship is an eternal friendship that will never end (1.21-24). Finally, this chapter concludes with the observation that while true friendship is exceedingly rare, the love of Christ has made such friendships plentiful within the church—a fact especially testified to by the church's many martyrs (1.25-30).

Text

Aelred's Prologue to His Readers

1. When I was still a schoolboy, I delighted in the pleasure of being with my friends more than in anything else; and among the habits and faults to which the young

---

1   Saint Aelred of Rievaulx, "Jesus at the Age of Twelve," in Treatises; The Pastoral Prayer, ed. M. Basil Pennington, Cistercian Fathers Series 2 (Kalamazoo, MI: Cistercian, 1971), 4.

are accustomed to endanger themselves, my mind gave itself totally to passionate affection, and devoted itself to love. The result was that to me nothing was more pleasant or more delightful or more useful than to seem to be loved and to love in return.[2]

2. And so, being tossed about among different loves and friendships, my mind was carried this way and that; and not knowing the law of true friendship, I was thus often deceived by what resembled friendship. Then, after some time, I acquired Cicero's famous book, *On Friendship*, and at once it seemed to me both useful in its weighty thoughts and pleasant in its agreeable eloquence.[3]

3. And although this book did not allow me to see myself as capable of the kind of friendship it described, I was still glad to have found a kind of principle for friendship, according to which I would be able to control my wandering loves and affection. But when it truly pleased the good Lord to correct my wandering, to raise me when I had fallen (*Pss 145:14; 146:8*), and to cleanse this leper with his healing touch (*Matt 8:2; Luke 7:22*), I abandoned worldly hope and entered a monastery.

4. And immediately I began to read the Holy Scriptures intently although in my prior life I would become bleary-eyed even before skimming over the Bible, and usually satisfied my gaze with mere fleshly shadows. Thus, as the

---

2   Aelred describes himself using the same language Augustine used in his spiritual autobiography (*Confessions*, 2.2). This is one of many places where Aelred has learned from wise Christian mentors and passes on their wisdom about friendship to us. For a thorough list, see the edition of *Spiritual Friendship* edited by Marsha Dutton.

3   For example, Cicero's "first law of friendship" states: "Ask of friends only what is honorable; do for friends only what is honorable" (*On Friendship*, 13.44).

Holy Scriptures grew sweet to me and that little bit of knowledge I had gained in the world grew more worthless in comparison, I remembered the things I had read in that little book of Cicero's, and I marveled then that what I had read did not seem as attractive to me as it once did.

5. For already then, nothing drew my affection entirely to itself which had not been sweetened by the name of Jesus, or flavored by the salt of the Holy Scriptures. And as I thought of these things, I constantly asked myself whether by chance what I had learned from Cicero could be supported by the authority of Scripture.

6. Thus since I wished to be able to love in a spiritual manner but could not, I read very much about friendship in the writings of the holy fathers. However, since I found no aid in them, I began to write about spiritual friendship and to set down for myself the rules of a pure and holy affection.

7. So I have divided this little work into three parts. In the first part I deal with the nature of friendship, noting its origin or cause; in the second I set forth its advantages and its excellence; and in the third I explain as clearly as I can how and among what sorts of people friendship is able to be preserved unbroken until the end.

> So I have divided this little work into three parts:
>
> The Nature of Spiritual Friendship
>
> The Advantages and Excellence of Spiritual Friendship
>
> How to Be Spiritual Friends

8. Therefore let anyone who profits from this book give thanks to God—and, since I am a sinner, let him also intercede on my behalf with Christ's

mercy. But if anyone should find what I have written to be redundant or useless, let him forgive my clumsiness, which forced me to hold back the flow of my thoughts in this meditation because of my engagement with other matters.

Start of the First Conversation and Introduction of the Friends: Aelred, Ivo, and Christ (1.1–4)

1. AELRED: Here we are, you and I, and I hope that Christ makes a third with us (*Matt 18:20*).[4] No one can interrupt us now, no one can spoil our friendly conversation; no one's voice or noise will break in upon this pleasant solitude of ours. So come now, dearest friend, reveal your heart and speak your mind. You have a friendly audience; say whatever you wish. And let us not be ungrateful for this time or for our opportunity and leisure.

> "Here we are, you and I, and I hope that Christ makes a third with us."

2. For just now, when I was sitting among the crowd of monks, they were all chattering on every side, and one was asking questions and another was arguing, and others were posing problems about the Scriptures, about ethics, about virtues and vices. You alone were silent. Now and then you looked up as though you were ready to make a point for the rest of us, but just when the words seemed on the tip of your tongue, you looked down again and kept silent. Occasionally you withdrew a short distance from our group and then returned, with a sad expression on your face. From all this I can only conclude that you have

---

4 Aelred's allusion to Matthew 18:20 emphasizes that Jesus promises to be present when two or three of his followers gather together. Aelred teaches us that an awareness of the presence of Jesus with two or more Christian friends is an important aspect of joyful, wise, and eternal friendship.

something on your mind, but you are afraid of the crowd, and desire privacy.

3. IVO: Yes, that's quite right, and I am very glad, since I know you care for me like a son. It must be the spirit of Christian love—no other—that has revealed my state of mind to you. And I wish that your regard for me would allow me this one favor: as often as you visit your spiritual children here, let me have you all to myself just once, apart from the others, so I can pour forth the turmoil of my heart without fear.

4. AELRED: I'll grant you that favor, and willingly! I am delighted to see that you are not given to arguing about empty and idle matters, but you are always engaged in some beneficial pursuit, something necessary to your spiritual development. So speak out without fear, and share all your cares and thoughts with a friend; so you may both learn and teach, give and receive, pour out your own soul but, at the same time, take in the soul of another.

Christian Friendship Is Better than Cicero's Friendship (1.5–10)

5. IVO: Indeed, I was prepared to learn, not to teach—not to give, but to receive, to pour out my own soul rather than to partake of yours. This is demanded by our respective ages; moreover, my lack of learning compels it, and my vows urge me to this end. But I do not wish to waste time foolishly on these matters when it is needed for other things: I want you to teach me something about spiritual friendship. I want to know its nature, its usefulness, the principle upon which it is founded, its end, whether all people are capable of it or what sort of people attain it, if not everybody can indeed, how is it possible to preserve

it unbroken, and to reach a holy end without any bothersome disagreements?

6. AELRED: I marvel that you think I am worthy to answer such questions, especially since nearly everyone agrees that these matters have been dealt with more than adequately by ancient authorities who were extraordinarily learned. But I marvel most of all, since you have spent your youth pursuing matters of this sort, and you have read Cicero's treatise *On Friendship*.[5] In this work Cicero has treated very fully and in a pleasant style everything that seems to have any bearing upon friendship.

7. IVO: I am not entirely ignorant of Cicero's work, since I have been accustomed from time to time to take great delight in it. But from the time when I began to recognize the sweetness of the Holy Scriptures and the honey-sweet name of Christ claimed my affection for itself, whatever lacked the salt of heavenly literature and the seasoning of that most pleasant name could not be tasty or attractive to me, no matter now cleverly argued what I read or heard seemed to me.

8. And so I wish to see for myself our most common assumptions about friendship proved by the authority of Scripture—even if these assumptions rest upon arguments that are in keeping with reason—and of course we must also provide scriptural proof of those other matters which the usefulness of this discussion on friendship demands. I also wish that you would treat more fully how that same friendship which ought to hold among us is both formed in Christ and preserved according to Christ and how

---

5   This work is available for free from the Internet History Sourcebook at https://sourcebooks.fordham.edu/ancient/cicero-friendship.asp.

friendship's goal and usefulness are ultimately referred to Christ. For it is clear that Cicero was unaware of the excellence of true friendship, since he was unaware of Christ, who is friendship's principle and goal.

9. AELRED: You have convinced me. But I confess that, since I almost feel as though I do not know myself, and I am afraid that my own abilities are not up to this task, I would rather not teach you about friendship but instead discuss this subject with you. And this only because you yourself have cleared the way for each of us, and have flooded the threshold of our inquiry with that most splendid light of scriptural illumination which should not allow us to wander off track, but instead should lead us by a sure path to the sure end of the question you have set before us.

Scripture Illuminates Our Understanding of Spiritual Friendship

10. For what can one say about friendship that is more sublime, more truthful, more useful, than that friendship will be shown to be formed in Christ, advanced according to Christ, and perfected by Christ? So come now; tell me what you think we ought to investigate first in the matter of friendship.

> *"Friendship will be shown to be formed in Christ, advanced according to Christ, and perfected by Christ."*

IVO: First I think we should explain the nature of friendship; otherwise, if we do not know what the course and contents of our investigation should explain, we may seem to be "painting in thin air."

Cicero's Definition of Friendship as a Conversation Starter (1.11–21)

11. AELRED: Cicero said, "Friendship is agreement on both human and divine affairs, combined with good will and affection."[6] Isn't his definition satisfactory to you?[7]

12. IVO: If this definition is satisfactory to you, I suppose it should satisfy me also.

13. AELRED: Will we therefore agree that whenever people are in perfect agreement about divine and human affairs and have the same desires along with good will and affection, then they have attained perfect friendship?

14. IVO: Why not? However, I do not understand what Cicero, as a pagan, means by the terms "good will" and "affection."

---

6 Cicero, *On Friendship*, 6.20.

7 Cicero's important definition will be repeated three more times: see 1.29, 1.46, and 3.8.

15. AELRED: Perhaps by "good will" he means the mental emotion of friendship, and by "affection" he means the expression of friendship in deeds. For each party in his own mind ought to esteem the same things—that is, their unanimity should be agreeable and dear to them; moreover, their subsequent actions in external matters ought to be well meaning and pleasant.

16. IVO: I confess that this definition pleases me; my only objection to it is that this definition is valid for both pagans and Jews, and even bad Christians as well. However, I must admit that I am persuaded that true friendship cannot exist among those who are without Christ.

17. AELRED: Whether Cicero's definition is lacking in any respect, or goes too far in another direction, will become clear enough for our purposes in what comes later. We will either reject it as insufficient, or accept it as requiring no further addition. Still, although the definition seems less than perfect to you, from it you will be able to understand in some way what friendship is.

18. IVO: I hope that I will not burden you, if I say that I will not be satisfied with this definition unless you reveal for me the true meaning of the word "friendship."

19. AELRED: I will grant you this favor, provided you forgive my ignorance and do not compel me to teach what I do not know. The word "friend" [amicus] is derived from "love" [amor], as it seems to me; and "friendship" [amicitia] is derived from "friend."[8]

However, love is an affection of the rational mind through which the mind seeks something for itself with desire and

---

8   Cicero, *On Friendship*, 8.24.

strives to enjoy that object of its desire. Love also enables the mind to enjoy the object of its desire with a certain internal pleasure, and once it has attained the object of its desire it embraces it and preserves it. I have already explained the passionate and emotional nature of love as well as I can in my essay *The Mirror of Charity*, with which I believe you are already familiar.

20. Further, a friend is called, as it were, the guardian of love—or, as some prefer to say, the "guardian of the soul" itself.[9] And so my friend must be the guardian of our mutual love, or even of my very soul, so that he will preserve in faithful silence all its secrets, and whatever he sees in it that is flawed he will correct or endure with all his strength. When I rejoice, he will rejoice; when I grieve, he will grieve with me (*Rom 12:15*); he will consider as his own everything that his friend experiences (*Acts 4:32*).

True Spiritual Friendship Is Eternal Friendship (1.21–24)

21. So friendship is that same virtue which joins minds in a bond of such esteem and pleasure, and they are made "one from many," as Cicero said.[10] So even worldly philosophers have classified friendship among those virtues which are eternal, rather than those things attributable to chance and change. Solomon appears to agree with this when he says in the Proverbs, "A friend loves at all times" (Prov 17:17). In saying this he makes it quite clear that friendship is eternal, provided it is true

---

9 The definition of a friend as a "soul-keeper" or "guardian of one's soul" (*animi custos*) has played an important role in Christian theology for many centuries. Gregory the Great (d. 604) used it in a sermon on John 15:12–16 (*Forty Gospel Homilies*, 27.4) and it was later popularized in Isidore of Seville's (d. 636) important dictionary, *Etymologies*, 10.4.

10 Cicero, *On Friendship*, 25.92.

friendship. However, if friendship ceases to exist, Solomon implies that it was never true friendship, however true it once seemed to be.

22. IVO: But why is it then that we read that serious enmity arises among the closest friends?

23. AELRED: We will discuss this more fully in its own place, God willing. Meanwhile, please do not believe that a man who was a true friend could ever harm someone whom he has once received into friendship. Moreover, neither should you believe that a man has ever tasted the delights of true friendship if he stops loving the friend he once loved, even if that friend did him some harm. For "a friend loves at all times" (Prov 17:17).

24. Even if he is corrected, even if he is hurt, even if he is handed over to be burned or is nailed to the cross, "a friend loves at all time" (Prov 17:17). Or as our own Jerome said, "Friendship which can fail was never true friendship."[11]

Is Spiritual Friendship Even Possible? (1.25–30)

25. IVO: Since there is in friendship such a great degree of perfection, it is no wonder that antiquity so rarely commended men as being true friends. For as Cicero said, "hardly three or four pairs of friends" are renowned

---

11 Jerome's (d. 420) letters to his friend Augustine (d. 430) provide a helpful window into spiritual friendship. Jerome valued loyalty in friendships more than any other trait. This quotation about friendship comes from a letter he wrote to his friend Rufinus when both were young men. It reads, "A friend is long sought, hardly found, and with difficulty kept . . . the friendship which can cease has never been real" (*Letters* 3.6). Jerome's letters can be read in *The Principle Works of St. Jerome*, vol. 6 of NPNF2, available at www.ccel.org.

in those many distant ages.[12] But if in our own age—that is, in the Christian era—friendship is so rare, then I think I am striving in vain to acquire a virtue which I confess I am already losing hope of attaining. I am so overwhelmed by its miraculous loftiness!

26. AELRED: "It is a great thing indeed to strive after great things," as someone once said.[13] Thus it is the mark of a virtuous mind always to meditate upon lofty and difficult things, so that it either attains or more clearly understands and recognizes that which it desires: so we should not believe that a man has made but little progress when he has recognized virtue and learned from that how far he is from virtue.

27. However, the Christian ought never to despair of attaining any virtue, since his ears echo daily with that saying from the gospel, "Seek, and you will find," and other sayings like it (Matt 7:7; *John* 16:24). So it is no wonder if among the Gentiles the followers of true virtue were rare, since they did not know the Lord who dispenses the virtues, of whom it is written, "The LORD of virtues, he is the King of glory" (Ps 24:10).[14]

28. Truly, I do not talk of merely three or four pairs of friends, as the pagans do, but I set before you a thousand pairs of friends, who by faith in the Lord were ready to die one for another—in short, to do as a matter of course what the pagans said or imagined a great miracle in the

---

12 Cicero, *On Friendship*, 4.15.

13 Julianus Pomerius, *The Contemplative Life*, 1.Prol.2.

14 Aelred is reading from a Latin Vulgate translation of Ps 23:10, which in English is Ps 24:10.

case of Pylades and Orestes.[15] Were they not powerful in the virtue of true friendship, even according to Cicero's definition, of whom it is written, "Now the full number of those who believed were of one heart and soul, and no one said that any of the things that belonged to him was his own, but they had everything in common" (Acts 4:32)?

29. How could Cicero's highest "agreement on both human and divine affairs, with affection and good will" fail to exist among those who were of "one heart and soul" (Acts 4:32)?[16] How many martyrs laid down their lives for their brothers! How many did not spare their possessions, their toil, even their own physical agony on the cross! I believe that you have read many times, and not without tears, of how that well known maiden of Antioch, rescued from the brothels by a certain soldier in a most admirable deceit, found in that soldier an ally in martyrdom shortly thereafter—and this the same man whom she had previously found to be a guardian of her chastity when she was in the brothel.[17]

30. I could give you many examples of this sort, except that the size of the topic prevents it, and our vow of

---

15 Cicero uses the famous Greek friends, Pylades and Orestes, who were willing to die for one another as an example of true friendship (*On Friendship*, 7.24). He identifies such friendships as "the rarest in the world, and all but superhuman" (*On Friendship*, 2.17).

16 Cicero, *On Friendship*, 6.20.

17 Aelred uses this story to illustrate how a Christian man and woman who were neither married, nor siblings, displayed true friendship with one another. It is one of a number of places where Aelred shows that Christian men and woman can be true friends, a fact that was denied by many (e.g. Aristotle) in the ancient world. The story of the two Christian martyrs can be found in one of Jerome's books (*On Virgins*, 2.4.22–32).

silence forbids us to use many examples. For Christ Jesus foretold these martyrs; he spoke, "yet they are more than can be told" (Ps 40:5). He said, "Greater love has no one than this, that someone lay down his life for his friends" (John 15:13).

Discussion Questions

In an age where "friends" on social media often number in the hundreds or even thousands, do you agree with Cicero that true "friends" are extremely rare? What about in the church? Do you think Aelred's claim that true friendship is much more common in the church still rings true today? Is Aelred's claim true in your church?

What do you think about Aelred's claim that Christian friendship is eternal? He suggests that a friendship that does not last was actually not a true Christian friendship because a friendship rooted in Christ will be never-ending. Have you experienced a friendship like this? Do you think the covenant friendship of Christian marriage might be an example of eternal friendship? Why or why not?

Aelred quotes a definition of a spiritual friend as one who is a "guardian of your soul." Have you experienced someone who you would describe as a "guardian of your soul"? What does it feel like to be in a relationship with someone you can trust completely with an unguarded heart?

If you were to sort your friendships into categories, how many would be "soul guardians"? How many would be "eternal friends"? How many would be simply acquaintances or just known names?

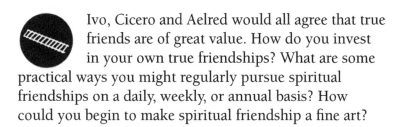

Ivo, Cicero and Aelred would all agree that true friends are of great value. How do you invest in your own true friendships? What are some practical ways you might regularly pursue spiritual friendships on a daily, weekly, or annual basis? How could you begin to make spiritual friendship a fine art?

CHRISTIAN MINISTRY

Chapter 2

The Definition and Origin of Spiritual Friendship (Book 1.31–71)

Chapter Summary

Do you think Christians can be friends with everyone? In this chapter Aelred and Ivo's conversation will help you discover why Aelred believes the answer while living here on earth is "no." He shows how there is a distinction between Christian love and spiritual friendship (1.31–32) and that if one does not love oneself, one cannot love a friend (1.35). Then Aelred explains the nature of three kinds of friendship: fleshly friendship, worldly friendship, and spiritual friendship (1.36–49). After explaining spiritual friendship's nature in contrast with these two lesser kinds of friendship, Aelred describes how spiritual friendship began at the creation of the world and flows directly from the Creator (1.50–56). He points to the first marriage, between Adam and Eve, as an example of the first human friendship and shows how this friendship indicates that

Adam and Eve are equal before God (1.57–60). Finally, Aelred points to the way wisdom and friendship are both important aspects of Christian love and thus are very closely related to one another (1.61–71). The conversation ends with Ivo being called away for a meal. Sadly, Ivo's death will prevent him from speaking in the remaining two conversations.

Text

The Difference between Love and Friendship (1.31–32)

31. IVO: Should we therefore believe that there is no difference between friendship and Christian love?

32. AELRED: Indeed, there is a great difference between them. For we have it on divine authority that more people ought to be received with Christian love than by the embrace of friendship. For the law of grace compels us to receive not only friends, but also enemies, with Christian love (*Matt 5:44; Luke 6:27–35*). However, we say that only they are friends to whom we are not afraid to entrust our hearts and everything that is in them—to those, in turn, who are bound to us by the same law of faith and security.

Spiritual Friendship Is Different from Other Kinds of Friendship (1.33–34)

33. IVO: But how many of those who live according to the world, and are unanimous in pursuing whatever vices are pleasing to themselves, are joined in a bond similar to that which binds Christians, and derive from that friendship a pleasure that surpasses the pleasure of the delights of this temporal world!

34. I hope that it will not be bothersome to you, if I believe that you should separate that friendship which is spiritual from the many other kinds of friendship. Spiritual friendship is to some extent involved with and obscured by other kinds of friendships, which can hinder those who desire spiritual friendship and are seeking after it, and entice them, if I might put it this way, to dissociate from fellowship. If you compare these different types of friendships, you will make spiritual friendship clearer and thus more desirable to me, and so make me more eager to attain it.

You Cannot Love a Friend if You Do Not Love Yourself (1.35)

35. AELRED: Worldly people falsely assume for themselves the outstanding name of friendship if they base their bond upon an agreement in vices, since he who does not love is not a friend. But he who loves iniquity does not love his fellow man, for "he who loves iniquity does not love, but rather hates his own soul."[1] And certainly he who does not love his own soul will in no way be capable of loving the soul of another.[2]

---

1 This is a possible reading of the Latin Vulgate translation of Ps 10:6, which in English is Ps 11:5).

2 Some twenty years before writing *Spiritual Friendship* Aelred wrote a longer book about love called *The Mirror of Charity*. In it he spends significant time explaining why Jesus' Great Commandment (Matt 22:37–40) requires a threefold love. Aelred tells us that if we diligently examine this command we "discover that three things must be loved: yourself, your neighbor, and God" (*Mirror of Charity*, 3.2.4).

How Spiritual Friendship Is Distinct from Other Types of Friendship (1.36–37)

36. And in connection with this, it follows that such a person boasts in the mere name of friendship, and is deceived by something that looks like friendship, rather than depending upon the truth. It may indeed be true that a person experiences something like the pleasure of a spiritual friendship in a friendship that is either stained by desire, or made foul by greed, or rendered impure by excess; but one must infer that, however much pleasure one can derive from an inferior friendship, to the degree that the friendship is more honorable, it is also more secure, and to the degree that the friendship is more pure, it is more pleasant, and to the degree that it is freer, it is happier.

37. Still, let us grant that, because of the similarity of emotions, even those friendships which are not true may be called friendships nonetheless, despite their being distinguished by certain marks from that friendship which is spiritual and therefore true.

"Fleshly Friendship" Is the First of the Three Kinds of Friendship (1.38–41)

38. So let us call one kind of friendship "fleshly" and another "worldly" and yet another "spiritual." And fleshly friendship is created by an agreement in vices, while hope of gain spurs on worldly friendship, and similarity of character, goals, and habits in life makes for a bond of friendship among good people.

39. The true impulse to fleshly friendship comes from that state of mind which, like a prostitute, directs its footsteps after every passerby (*Ezek 16:25*), following its

ears and eyes, lusting through the highways and byways (*Num 15:39*). Through these means—that is, through the eyes and the ears—the image of beautiful and desirable objects is brought all the way into the mind itself; and the mind considers itself happy if it can enjoy these things at its pleasure, although without an accomplice in its pleasure it thinks itself less happy.[3]

40. Then, by gesture, nod, words, and indulgence, one spirit is made captive by another, and the one is enkindled by the other, and they catch fire together as one. The result of this wretched agreement, once made, is that the one will do or suffer anything that is criminal or sacrilegious on behalf of the other; both partners think that nothing is sweeter than their friendship, and that nothing is more just. By agreeing on "likes and dislikes" they believe they are guided by the rules of friendship.[4]

41. And so this sort of friendship is not undertaken with forethought, nor approved by judgment, nor ruled by

---

3   Stories can help us picture examples of "fleshly friendships." A biblical example is found in Amnon and Jonadab (2 Sam 13:3–5). Other examples include the story of Augustine and his teenage friends stealing and destroying pears for fun or a fictional example such as the two friends, Tub and Frank, who support one another in vices like secret gluttony and pedophilia. See Augustine of Hippo, *The Confessions*, trans. Maria Boulding, WSA (Hyde Park, NY: New City, 1997), 2.4.9; Tobias Wolff, "Hunters in the Snow," in *Perrine's Literature: Structure, Sound, and Sense*, eds. Greg Johnson and Thomas R. Arp, 12th ed. (Stamford, CT: Wadsworth, 2015), 79–93.

4   Aelred refers to a famous speech by Catiline who tried to overthrow the Roman Republic in 63 BC. When speaking to his supporters, Catiline is reported to have said, "I perceive that you and I hold the same view of what is good and evil; for agreement in likes and dislikes—this, and this only, is what constitutes true friendship" (Sallust, *The War With Catiline*, trans. John C. Rolfe, Loeb Classical Library (Cambridge, MA: Harvard University Press, 1931), 4.20. Aelred refers to Catliline's definition five times in *Spiritual Friendship* (see also 1.48, 2.28, 3.11, 3.124).

reason; rather it follows the impetus of emotion and is carried away through life's highways and byways. It follows no mean, nor does it aim at what is honorable; it does not distinguish between what is useful and useless, but in everything it follows a course that is thoughtless, indiscriminating, flighty, and excessive. For this reason this sort of friendship consumes itself as though urged on by furies, or else it is dissolved with the same flightiness with which it was initiated.

"Worldly Friendship" Is the Second of the Three Kinds of Friendship (1.42–44)

42. Worldly friendship, on the other hand, is created by desire for temporal goods and things. It is always full of deceit and deception; in it there is nothing certain, nothing constant, nothing secure. For this reason it is the sort of friendship that changes with fortune, and follows money (*Eccl 9:11–12*).

43. Thus it is written:

> For there are friends who are such when it suits them, but they will not stand by you in time of trouble (*Sir 6:8, NRSV*).[5]

Take away the hope of gain, and immediately he will cease to be a friend. This sort of friendship one of the poets mocks in this elegant couplet:

---

5   Aelred is quoting from the Wisdom of Sirach, called Ecclesiasticus in the Latin Bible that Aelred used. As part of the Apocrypha, Sirach is considered canonical by Eastern Orthodox, Roman Catholic, Ethiopian Orthodox, and Syriac church traditions. Evangelicals follow Martin Luther in viewing the book not as Scripture but as a helpful spiritual classic. Sirach places a major emphasis on friendship, and Aelred quotes from it thirteen times in *Spiritual Friendship*.

A friend not of persons but of wealth is he,
Who for better is faithful, and for worse flees.[6]

44. Nevertheless the beginning of this sort of flawed friendship often starts many on the road to a certain element of true friendship. This is the case especially with those who first enter a bond of friendship in the outward hope of common gain while they keep faith with themselves in the expectation of outstripping their associates in riches; in human affairs, at least, they attain the greatest pleasure and mutual agreement (*Luke 16:9*). Still, that which is undertaken and preserved for the sake of temporal advantage can in no way be called true friendship.

"Spiritual Friendship" Is the Third and True Kind of Friendship (1.45–49)

45. For spiritual friendship, which is what we mean by true friendship, should be desired not with a view to any worldly good, nor for any reason extrinsic to itself, but from the worthiness of its own nature, and the feeling of the human heart, so that it offers no advantage or reward other than itself.

46. So the Lord says in the Gospel of John, "I chose you . . . that you should go and bear fruit," that is, so that you might love one another (*John 15:16–17*). For in this true friendship one makes progress by bettering oneself, and one bears fruit by experiencing the enjoyment of this increasing degree of perfection. And so spiritual friendship is born among good people through the similarity of their

---

6   Aelred is quoting from "Letters from the Black Sea", a poem by a Roman poet named Ovid who was alive at the time of Christ. We could also give "worldly friends" the title "fair-weather friends."

characters, goals, and habits in life. This is what Cicero meant by "agreement with good will and affection" in matters both divine and human.[7]

47. This definition seems to me to be sufficient to express what friendship is, provided by friendship we mean what we commonly take to be Christian love, so that we may exclude every vice from friendship. Good will, however, should be expressed as that feeling of love which is moved in our hearts by a certain enjoyment.

48. Where such friendship is, there is certainly that "agreement on likes and dislikes" that we mentioned earlier, and indeed this agreement is stronger to the extent that it is more sincere, and more pleasant to the extent that it is more holy.[8] Where friends love each other in this manner, they can desire nothing which is not fitting, and they can wish to avoid nothing which will advance their friendship.

49. Surely prudence guides this friendship, justice rules it, courage watches over it, and moderation tempers it. We will address each of these matters in its own place; now, however, please tell me whether you think I have sufficiently dealt with your first matter of concern, the nature of friendship.

The Origin of Friendship (1.50–56)

50. IVO: What you have said is sufficient; I cannot think of anything further which I would ask you on this particular

---

7   Cicero, *On Friendship*, 6.20. This is the second of four times that Aelred uses Cicero's definition of friendship.

8   See *Spiritual Friendship*, 1.40.

matter. But before we go on to other things, I would like to know where friendship among mortals first came from. Is it natural or accidental, or does it arise from some necessity? Was it imposed upon the human race by some statute or law? For indeed, our experience with it is what makes it attractive to us.

51. AELRED: It seems to me that nature herself first stamped human minds with the emotion of friendship, and then experience increased it, and finally the authority of law put it in order.[9] For God, being the highest power and the highest good, is self-sufficient with regard to what is good, since he himself is his own good, his own joy, his own glory, his own blessing.

52. Nor does he need anything which is external to himself, neither man, nor angel, nor heaven, nor earth, nor anything which is in these. Indeed, every creature proclaims to him, "You are my Lord, since you need none of my goods" (Ps 16:2).[10] Not only is God self-sufficient; he is himself the sufficiency of all created things, granting some mere existence, granting others sentience, and granting still others knowledge, while himself remaining the cause of all existing things, the life of all sentient things, and the knowledge of all knowledgeable things.

53. And so God himself, as the Highest Nature, established all natures, put all things in their proper place, separately distributed all things to their proper

---

9   For Aelred, "nature herself" points to the God who authored nature. Thus, friendship is part of human nature because God designed it as an important aspect of humanity.

10   Aelred paraphrases Ps 16:2 here.

times. But because his eternal reason demanded it, he wished all his creatures to be joined together in peace, and for community to exist between them. And thus all his creatures are allotted a certain vestige of unity from him who is supremely and purely one. For this reason he left no class of his creatures alone, but he linked them together in a certain community out of diversity.

54. For if we begin with insensible things, what earth, or what river, brings forth stones of just one kind? Or what forest produces just one kind of tree? Thus even among insensible things a certain love of community, as it were, shines forth, since none of these things exists alone, but they all are created and exist with a certain community of type. And indeed, who can easily say how much the type of friendship and the image of community and love shine forth among sentient beings?[11]

55. Indeed, although in all else irrational creatures are set apart from humans by their very lack of reason, in this one respect they imitate the human spirit, in that they almost appear to be led by reason: so they follow each other, they play with each other, in their movements and noises they express and give evidence of their mutual affection. So avidly and happily do they enjoy their common community, that they appear to care for nothing more than those things we associate with friendship.

---

11 Sentient being – a being with senses that is able to recognize and respond to sensations like touch, sight, hearing, touch, taste, or smell.

56. So even among the angels divine wisdom saw to it that not just one, but many were created, among whom community was welcome and the sweetest love created a unity of will and affection. This was so that, once differences in rank were recognized, there would be no occasion for envy—but *agape* love intervened to prevent this. And so sheer numbers banished solitude and mutual participation in *agape* love increased the happiness of the many.

Men and Women Are Equal and Created for Friendship (1.57–60)

57. And when God created mankind afterward, in order to commend more highly the good conferred by human society he said, "It is not good that the man should be alone; I will make him a helper fit for him" (Gen 2:18). Certainly divine virtue did not simply form this helper from similar or even from the same material, but woman was created expressly as an incentive for Christian love and friendship, from the very substance of the man himself. And so it is beautiful that the second created being was taken from the side of the first so that nature might teach that all are equals, as it were "collateral."[12] In human affairs there is to be neither superior nor inferior; this is the appropriate mark of friendship.

> "In human affairs there is to be neither superior nor inferior; this is the appropriate mark of friendship."

---

12 Collateral – a person having the same descent in a family, but by a different line. Aelred is also making a pun in the Latin since the word "side" is *latus*, and Eve came from Adam's side.

The First Spiritual Friendship Was a Marriage

58. So from the very beginning nature impressed upon human minds the emotional desire for friendship and love, a desire which mankind's inner sense of love increased with a certain taste of sweetness. But after the fall of the first humans, when love grew cold and greed had crept in and made mankind prefer private property to the common good, avarice and envy corrupted the splendor of friendship and love, and brought disputes, rivalries, hatred, and suspicion to our corrupted human nature.

59. Then those who were good began to distinguish between love and friendship, noticing that affection ought to be given even to those who are enemies and perverse,

although among the good and the bad there can be no
fellowship of wills or counsel. And so friendship, which
like love was first preserved among all and by all, remained
among a few good people according to natural law. These
good people, seeing the holy laws of faith and fellowship
violated by the many, joined themselves together by a closer
bond of affection and friendship, and so among the evils
which they saw and felt they rested in the pleasure of
mutual love.

60. Nevertheless, even those whose unrighteousness
obliterated all sense of virtue still did not lose their sense
of reason, which in turn prevented them from entirely
losing the desire for friendship and fellowship. The result
was that without friends, riches could afford no delight
to the greedy man, nor fame to the ambitious, nor pleasure
to the sensuous. Even among the worst of people there
are certain agreements, and even sworn bonds of fellowship.
However, though these agreements have been cloaked
with that most attractive name of friendship, it has long
been felt that they should be distinguished both by law
and by precept from true friendship, so that when one
looked for true friendship, one would not be caught
unawares in the other because of a certain resemblance
between the two.

Friendship and Wisdom (1.61–71)

61. So the authority of law regulates the same friendship
which nature begins and custom strengthens. Thus it is
abundantly clear that natural friendship is like virtue,
wisdom, and other qualities which are both sought and
preserved, as natural goods, for their own sake; each

person who attains them uses them well, and no one abuses them absolutely.

62. IVO: But I must ask, don't many people abuse wisdom, who desire to please men from it, or who are overweening in their pride in the wisdom with which they have been endowed, or surely they abuse wisdom who consider it a thing for sale, and think righteousness a commodity to be bought?

63. AELRED: In this matter you will be satisfied with what Augustine said: "He who takes pleasure in himself, takes pleasure in a fool; for he is indeed a fool who pleases himself."[13] Truly he who is a fool is unwise, and he who is unwise, is unwise by virtue of not having wisdom at all. How therefore does one who has no wisdom use it badly? So also chastity that is prideful cannot be considered a virtue, for pride itself, which is a fault, makes that which is considered a virtue conform to itself, so that that which was previously a virtue is turned into a vice.

64. IVO: But—and I speak with your indulgence—it does not seem to me to follow, when you link wisdom to friendship, since there is no comparison between the two of them.

65. AELRED: Even though degrees of comparison, like "smaller" and "larger," or "good" and "better," or "weaker" and "stronger," are not equivalent, still in the matter of virtues such degrees of comparison are often quite closely connected; that is, things which differ from each other

---

13 Aelred appears to be quoting from one of Augustine's sermons. Today more than 540 of Augustine's sermons have survived and continue to be read with profit.

by degree are still close to each other by a similarity they may share. So widowhood is a near neighbor to virginity, and marital sexual faithfulness to widowhood;[i] and although there are great differences between these virtues in that with respect to which they are virtues, there is some degree of conformity among them.

66. And so it cannot be said that marital sexual faithfulness is not a virtue simply because the abstinence of a widow exceeds it; indeed, sanctified singleness from youth is preferable to both marital sexual faithfulness and abstinent widowhood, but even so it does not render either of the other virtues worthless.[ii] So if you carefully examine the things we have said about friendship, you will find that friendship is so close to wisdom, or even filled with wisdom, that I would almost say that friendship is nothing else but wisdom.

67. IVO: I must confess that I am at a loss, and I do not think that you can easily persuade me that your view is correct.

68. AELRED: Don't you remember that Scripture says, "A friend loves at all times" (Prov 17:17)? And if I remember correctly Jerome also says, "Friendship which can end was never true friendship."[14] I have already showed more than sufficiently that friendship cannot even exist without love. Therefore, since eternity thrives in friendship, and truth shines forth in it, and love likewise becomes pleasant through friendship, you be the judge whether you should separate the name of wisdom from these three.

---

14 Jerome, *Letter*, 3.6.

"But what does all of this mean? Shall I say of friendship what Jesus' friend, the Apostle John, said of love, that 'God is friendship'?"

69. IVO: But what does all of this mean? Shall I say of friendship what Jesus' friend, the Apostle John, said of love, that "God is friendship" (1 John 4:16)?

70. AELRED: That would indeed be unusual, and it does not have any scriptural authority. However, I do not hesitate at all to ascribe to friendship that which follows from love, since (as it were) "whoever abides" in friendship "abides in God, and God abides in him" (1 John 4:16). This is a matter you will see more clearly when we discuss the effects and usefulness of friendship; but now, if I have exercised my poor wit enough on the question of what friendship is, let us save for another time the other matters which you have asked me to explain.

71. IVO: An excessive delay would be very bothersome to me in my eagerness to learn about friendship, but now is the time when we must go to dinner, from which we are not permitted to be absent. And not only that, but many others have burdensome expectations of you, which compel you to give them your time.

Discussion Questions

 Aelred writes that "woman was created expressly as an incentive for Christian love and friendship, from the very substance of the man himself. And so it is beautiful that the second created being was taken from the side of the first so that nature might teach that all are equals" (1.57). Aelred's teaching about the equality of men and women may seem obvious now, but it was revolutionary in ancient times. Thinking about your own culture, what does spiritual friendship between men and women look like? Is it only possible between a married husband and wife? Is it possible for single men and women to be spiritual friends? What about a married spouse and someone of the opposite gender? What wisdom does your church's tradition and experience bring to these questions?

 Aelred thinks it is very important to understand the difference between Christian love (*agape*) and Christian friendship (1.31–32). Have you considered this distinction before? Do you agree that while Christians are called to love all people, we can only trust our hearts to a few (1.32)?

How do you feel about Aelred's statement that we are not loving ourselves if we allow sin to continue in our life (1.35)? What about his further claim that if we do not love ourselves, we will not be able to be true spiritual friends to another? Do you find this statement encouraging? Discouraging? Does it increase or decrease your desire to become the kind of person who can develop strong spiritual friendships?

 Aelred says, "So if you carefully examine the things we have said about friendship, you will find that friendship is so close to wisdom, or even filled with wisdom, that I would almost say that friendship is nothing else but wisdom" (1.66). Do you agree with Aelred that a wise life and a life full of true spiritual friends are almost the same thing? In what ways is he right? In what ways would you want to qualify or challenge his claim?

 Aelred says that "spiritual friendship is born among good people through the similarity of their characters, goals, and habits in life" (1.46). What habits might spiritual friends share that would encourage their love for God and for one another? Consider spiritual disciplines like Scripture memorization, *lectio divina*, a shared Bible reading plan, times of prayer, accountability groups, conversation, spending time together in creation, walking, hiking, or others that come to mind.

Chapter 3

The Advantages and Excellence of Spiritual Friendship (Book 2.1–27)

Chapter Summary

What spiritual discipline do you think is most helpful for growing into spiritual maturity? In this chapter, Aelred's second conversation (Book 2), we discover Aelred's claim that spiritual friendship is the best spiritual discipline for producing spiritual maturity. The chapter begins with sad news: Aelred's close friend from the previous conversation, Ivo, died some years previously. This second conversation introduces Walter, a somewhat arrogant and socially awkward man, whom Aelred nevertheless embraces as a spiritual friend (2.1–7). After Walter reads Aelred and Ivo's earlier conversation, he asks Aelred to explain the advantages of spiritual friendship (2.8–13). Aelred shows a number of advantages, but the most important benefit is that friendship as a spiritual discipline provides a reliable path to growing into spiritual maturity (2.14–15).

At this point a new friend, Gratian, arrives. Aelred explains his thesis—spiritual friendship begins with Christ, grows with Christ, and reaches its destination in spending an eternity together as friends of Christ (2.18–20). Aelred uses Solomon's description of a kiss between a husband and wife in the Song of Songs, as an example of three levels of friendship (2.21–25). The first level of friendship is illustrated by the bliss of a physical kiss; the second by the joy found in sharing one's soul in an unguarded way with a friend; and the third by the unutterable joy of conscious union with Christ (2.26–27).

Text

Friends Attend to One Another (2.1–3)

1. AELRED: Come now, brother, give in: tell me why, just a few moments ago, while I was dealing with worldly men and their affairs, you were sitting all alone, removed from us some distance. And just now you were shooting glances this way and that, rubbing your forehead with your hand, and running your fingers through your hair, with your face itself betraying your anger that something has happened to you against your will. So speak.

2. WALTER: That is indeed the case. For who could patiently put up with it all day, when "Pharaoh's taskmasters" (Exod 5:14) have you all to themselves? You are especially obliged to me, but I can't seem to have even a word with you.

3. AELRED: This is the sort of thing we must do for those whose favors we desire or whose malice we fear. But now that they're all gone, our solitude is as welcome to me as the previous bustle was bothersome. For "hunger is the

best seasoning for food," and neither honey nor anything else gives as much taste to wine as thirst does to mere water.[1] And so perhaps our conversation here will be like spiritual food or drink for you, more pleasant since the heat which brought it about was more severe. So come, reveal what made you anxious just now; don't hesitate to speak freely.

A Friend's Conversation Provides Rich Spiritual Food

The Rediscovery of Aelred's Written Conversation with Ivo on Spiritual Friendship (2.4–7)

4. WALTER: I'll do that. For if I wished to make excuses now because of the very brief time those men have left us, I would appear to make our remaining time even shorter.

---

1   Aelred is quoting a proverb from Xenophon (d. 354 BC), a famous Greek general and one of Socrates' students.

So please tell me, has it slipped your mind, or do you yet remember, what passed between you and your friend Ivo on the topic of spiritual friendship? What questions did he ask you? How far did you go in your explanation, and what did you put in writing on these matters?

5. AELRED: Ah, the memory of that most dear man, and of his constant esteem and affection, are still always with me! Although he is no longer living among men, he brought so much to our relationship that he seems to my mind never to have died. For he is always there with me: his pious visage shining forth, his laughing eyes, his pleasant conversation, all of which are so agreeable that I sometimes think I have either passed on with him to better things, or else he is still involved in earthly affairs with me here below (*Heb 12:1*).[2] But you know that many years have passed since I lost the bit of paper on which I wrote down his questions and my answers on spiritual friendship.

6. WALTER: Yes, I'm well aware of that. But, to tell the truth, all my desire and impatience in this matter come from this: I heard from some brothers that your notes on spiritual friendship were found and returned to you three days ago. I beg you, show them to me. I ask you as a child would ask his father; for my spirit will not rest until I see them all and take note of what is lacking in your discussion, and bring to the scrutiny of their author those matters which either my own wit or some secret inspiration will point out for examination, for rejection or acceptance, or for exposition.

---

2 Just as Jesus was present, yet invisible, in the first conversation on friendship, now Jesus and Ivo are both invisible, yet present, participants in this second conversation about friendship.

7. AELRED: You have my permission to examine the document but I want you to read it alone, and not to bring it to the eye of the public. I may later come to think that some parts of this work ought to be deleted; other parts might have to be added and, indeed, there may be many errors which should be corrected.

So (Soul) What? What Is the Fruit or Value of Spiritual Friendship? (2.8–13)

[The conversation between Walter and Aelred is picked up again at some later time later after Walter has had a chance to read the notes from Aelred and Ivo's earlier conversation about friendship (Chapters 1 and 2). Walter and Aelred will soon be joined by Gratian, and the three friends will be the speaking participants in all the remaining conversations.]

8. WALTER: Here I am, ready to hear what you have to say. And I'm all the more eager, since what you wrote about friendship is very pleasant indeed. Therefore, since I have read your excellent discussion on the nature of friendship, I want you to help me to attain a more perfect knowledge of what the benefits of friendship are to those who cultivate it. For friendship is a very great thing, as you appear to have shown by sure arguments; but it will be sought out more ardently only when its goal and its benefits are recognized.

> "Friendship is a very great thing ... but it will be sought out more ardently only when its goal and its benefits are recognized."

9. AELRED: I do not presume that I can explain such a matter in a way that is worthy of its great dignity. For in human affairs there is no goal that is holier than friendship, nothing more useful, nothing more difficult to find, nothing that is sweeter to experience, nothing more enjoyable to

maintain. For friendship bears fruit in this life as well as in the life to come (*1 Tim 4:8*).

10. Friendship establishes all the virtues by means of its own charm, and it strikes down vices by its own excellence; it moderates difficulty and it imposes order upon prosperity. The result of friendship's activity in these spheres is that it is impossible for mortal men to experience pleasure without at least one friend. A human being without a friend is like a beast: for he lacks someone with whom he can share his joy in prosperity and his sadness in adversity (*Rom 12:15*), to whom he may unburden his mind when he is preoccupied, with whom he may talk whenever he has had a particularly sublime or illuminating insight.

11. "Woe to him who is alone when he falls and has not another to lift him up" (Eccl 4:10). That person is completely alone who has no friend.

But what happiness, what security, what pleasure it is to have a friend "with whom you would dare to speak just as you would speak to yourself!"[3] You would not fear to confide to a friend about your failings, nor would you blush to reveal to him your spiritual progress; and will you not entrust your plans for the future to the one to whom you have committed all the secrets of your heart? What then can be more pleasant than to unite one mind with another, and "to make one from two"?[4] Among friends no boasting or suspicion need be feared, nor need one partner be saddened to receive correction from his

---

3　Cicero, *On Friendship*, 6.22.

4　In this paragraph Aelred quotes from both Cicero and Ambrose to show that a good friend doubles joys and halves sorrows.

friend, nor should the one note the other for having been praised and censure him for adulation.

12. "Faithful friends," said the Wise Man, "are life-saving medicine" (Sir 6:16). And this is quite the case. For medicine is no more healthy or effective or excellent for our bodily wounds, than it is for us to have a friend who shows compassion to our every misfortune and shares our joy in every good thing. According to the Apostle, such friends bear one another's burdens, shoulder to shoulder with each other (Gal 6:2)—except that each one bears his own injuries more lightly than those of his friend.

13. So friendship "makes favorable circumstances even more splendid, and adverse circumstances more bearable by sharing them."[5] Therefore a friend is the best "life-saving medicine" (Sir 6:16).

And even the Gentiles agreed with this sentiment: "We depend on fire and water no more than we depend on friends."[6] In every act, in every pursuit; in certainty and in doubt; in every event, whatever fortune brings; in private and in public; in every deliberation, at home and in the world: friendship is everywhere welcome, friends are necessary, and their favor is always found to be useful. And so friends, as Cicero says, are there for each other "even when they are absent, are rich even when they are needy, and strong even when they are weak; and—though it is rather difficult to put into words—they live on even after they have died" (Sir 6:16).[7]

---

5 Cicero, On Friendship, 6.22.

6 Ibid.

7 Aelred quotes from Sir 6:16 and Cicero (On Friendship, 6:22–23) to show that friendship is essential to a good life.

Friendship Is a Spiritual Discipline: A Path Leading toward God (2.14–15)

14. Therefore, to the rich, friendship is like glory; to exiles, it is like a homeland; to the poor, it is like a family fortune; to the sick, it is like medicine; to the dead, it is like life; to the healthy, it is like grace; to the weak, it is like strength; to the strong, it is like a prize. For "such honor, memory, praise and desire follow" friends, that their lives are judged to be praiseworthy and their deaths are precious.[8]

And, in this respect, friendship excels everything I've just said, for friendship is a path that leads very close to the perfection which consists of the enjoyment and knowledge of God, such that a man who is a friend of man is made into a friend of God, according to what the Savior said in the gospel: "No longer do I call you servants . . . but I have called you friends" (John 15:15).

15. WALTER: Your speech has truly admonished me—it has whetted my mind's appetite for friendship—that I hardly consider myself really alive while I lack the diverse fruits of so great a good as a friendship. But I wish that you would explain for me more fully that result of friendship which you mentioned last; I am quite taken with it, as it has almost made me forget earthly conceptions of friendship. I mean your point about friendship being the best path to perfection.[9]

---

8 Cicero, *On Friendship*, 7.23.

9 Perfection – spiritual maturity, or complete conformity to Christ. See also Eph 4:11–16.

Gratian Arrives for the "Feast" of Friendship (2.16–17)

16. And here comes our friend Gratian, just in time; I could rightly call him friendship's child,[iii] since he lives "to be loved and to love."[10] It will be good for him to hear our conversation, since he is so excessively eager for friendship; thus he may not be deceived by something similar to friendship and take false friendship for true, or a contrived friendship for one that is solid, or a friendship according to the flesh for one that is spiritual.

17. GRATIAN: I thank you for your kindness, brother, that you have now allowed one who was not invited, but who rather impudently intrudes himself, to join your spiritual banquet. For if you seriously thought I should be called "friendship's child," and were not being playful, I should have been invited into the conversation at its very beginning. Then I would not have had to set aside my modesty and show my eagerness. But you, father, go on where you had begun, and for my sake put something on the table of this feast.[11] So, even if I am not filled up as he is (who has devoured who knows how many courses and only now invites me for the leftovers of which he is tired), I may be somewhat satisfied.[12]

---

10 Aelred described himself as a teenager with these same words (Prol. 1) which he had borrowed from Augustine's description of himself as a teenager. Augustine, *Confessions*, 2.2.

11 The image of friendship as a feast points to the marriage feast of the Lamb where friendship will be enjoyed eternally. For more on this theme see Paul D. O'Callaghan, *The Feast of Friendship* (Wichita, KS: Eighth Day, 2002), 133–137.

12 Dear reader, if you have not yet noted the fun these friends are having as they talk together, please do so now. Aelred wants us to see that friends can joke and laugh together—even when discussing serious topics.

Spiritual Friendship Begins with Christ, Grows through Christ, and Reaches Maturity in Christ (2.18–20)

18. AELRED: Have no fear on that account, my son. There is still much to say about the good we derive from friendship; if some philosopher were to pursue this matter thoroughly, you would think that we had said nothing thus far.

Now, as to how friendship is a path to the love and knowledge of God, here is something to think about. Because there is nothing dishonorable in friendship, there is in friendship nothing made up, nothing faked, and whatever friendship is, it is both voluntary and true and holy. And this is also itself a quality of Christian love.

19. In this respect indeed friendship exhibits a special token, in that among those who are joined to each other by the bond of friendship all things are felt to be pleasing, all things seem secure, sweet and delightful.

Therefore, from the perfection of Christian love, we are able to esteem those who are otherwise burdensome or unpleasant to us; we take account of their interests honestly, not disingenuously, not deceitfully, but truly and without being compelled to do so. However, we do not admit them to the privacy of our friendship.

20. And so in friendship are joined honesty and agreeableness, truth and pleasantness, sweetness and will, affection and action. All of these qualities come together in Christ, they are advanced through Christ, and in Christ they are perfected.

Therefore, if we begin with Christ, the ascent to friendship does not seem too difficult or unnatural, since it is Christ who inspires the love with which we esteem a friend, Christ who even points out to us the friend whom we love. So agreeableness follows agreeableness, sweetness follows sweetness, and affection follows affection.

The First Kiss: A Blending of Physical Breath Making One (2.21–25)

21. And so one friend clings to another in the spirit of Christ, and thus makes with him "one heart and soul" (Acts 4:32; 1 Cor 6:17), and so ascending together with his friend through the paths of love to the friendship of Christ, "a friend becomes one with him in the one kiss of the Spirit."[iv] A kind of holy intent yearns after this kiss and says, "Let him kiss me with the kisses of his mouth!" (Song 1:2).[13]

---

13 Today's readers may not be aware that the Song of Songs is perhaps the most important biblical book for understanding historical Christian spirituality. Besides describing the loving friendship between an earthly husband and wife, many read the book as describing Christ as heavenly groom and either the church or the believer's soul as bride. Aelred's good friend, Bernard of Clairvaux (d. 1153), gave eighty-six sermons on the Song of Songs with this focus on Christ and believers joined in spiritual marriage. Aelred's comments on the Song of Songs should be understood in relation to Bernard's sermons, available in multiple English translations under the title *Commentary on the Song of Songs*. Bernards' *Commentary on the Song of Songs* continues to be required reading for Cistercian and Trappist Christian communities (more than four thousand members as of 2021) and the text was one of A. W. Tozer's core thirty-five spiritual classics which he recommended to evangelicals for regular and repeated readings.

Friends Cling to One Another in the Spirit of Christ

22. Let us consider the propriety of this fleshly kiss, so that we may pass from fleshly things to spiritual things, from the human to the divine. The life of mankind is sustained by two types of nourishment, food and air. Without food a person is able to live for a while, but without air this is not possible for even an hour. So while we live, we take in air through the mouth and exhale it again. What is exhaled and inhaled is called "breath."[14]

23. Thus, in one kiss two spirits[15] meet one another, and they are mixed together and so made one. From this mingling of spirits there grows up a kind of mental

---

14 Aelred's wordplay is lost in translation as the Latin word used here, *spiritus*, can be translated as either "spirit" or "breath."

15 Or "breaths."

agreeableness, which elicits and joins together the affection of those who kiss.

24. So we might talk of different kinds of kisses: the kiss of the "flesh," the kiss of the "spirit," and the kiss of "understanding."[v]

A kiss of the flesh is made by a pressing together of lips, while a kiss of the spirit is made by a coming together of two souls, and the kiss of understanding results from the outpouring of grace through the spirit of God.[vi]

The kiss of the flesh is to be neither offered nor received, except for definite and honorable reasons—for example, as a sign of reconciliation, in place of words, when two people who had been mutual enemies become friends (*Luke 23:12*); or as a sign of peace, as when those who are about to partake of communion in church show their inner peace by means of an external kiss; or as a sign of affection, such as is permitted to happen between a husband and wife, or such as is offered and accepted by friends who have long been apart; or as a sign of catholic unity, such as when a guest is received.[16]

25. But just as many people abuse water, fire, iron, food, and air, which are naturally good, and convert them into a means of protecting their own cruelty and lust, so the shameful and perverse strive, after a fashion, to season their own disgraceful acts even with the kiss of the flesh,

---

16 The early church greeted one another with kisses on the lips (1 Cor 16:20; 2 Cor 13:12; 1 Thess 5:26). The "holy kiss" (Rom 16:16) or "kiss of love" (1 Pet 5:14) emphasized that believers were all members of one family. Some scholars today argue along similar lines to Aelred, stating that the sharing of breath/spirit in a physical kiss was used to symbolize the sharing of the Holy Spirit for the early Christians (Lawrence Phillips, *The Ritual Kiss in Early Christian Worship*. Cambridge: Grove, 1996).

a good which natural law instituted as a sign of the good things I just mentioned. So greatly do they befoul the kiss with their shamefulness, that to be kissed by one of these people is nothing less than to be corrupted. Every honest person knows how this is to be hated, abominated, fled, and opposed.[17]

The Second Kiss: A Blending of Souls Making One (2.26)

26. Further, the kiss of the spirit is proper for friends who are bound under one law of friendship. For it comes about not through physical contact of the mouth but through mental affection not by a joining of the lips but by a mingling of two spirits;[18] and from the Spirit of God that purifies all things and imparts a heavenly savor from its participation in the act.

It would not be inappropriate for me to call this sort of kiss the kiss of Christ, although he offers it not from his own mouth but from the mouth of another, inspiring that most holy affection in those who love one another, so that it appears to them as though one spirit indwells many different bodies. So they may say with the prophet, "Behold, how good and how pleasant it is when brothers dwell in unity!" (Ps 133:1).

---

17 For similar warnings about the dangers of a holy kiss in church becoming poluted, see *Apostolic Tradition* 18.2–4 (c. 400) and Clement of Alexandria (d. 215), *Christ the Teacher*, 3.81.1–82.1.

18 The wording here is similar to Aelred's wording when giving a eulogy for his friend Simon: "How have you been torn from my embrace, withdrawn from my kisses, removed before my eyes? I embraced you dear brother, not in the flesh but in the heart. I used to kiss you not with a touch of the lips but with attachment of mind. . . . You . . . linked with me . . . in the inner depths of your soul." Aelred of Rievaulx, *The Mirror of Charity* 1.34.109.

The Third Kiss: A Blending of Soul with the Spirit of Christ Making One (2.27)

27. Therefore, the mind becomes accustomed to this kind of kiss, and does not doubt that this pleasure comes totally from Christ; indeed, the mind reflects and says to itself, "O if only He Himself would come!" It longs for that kiss of understanding, and with the greatest desire exclaims, "Let him kiss me with the kisses of his mouth!" (Song 1:2), so that, with all earthly affections lessened and with all thoughts and desires which are of the world laid to rest, he delights only in the kiss of Christ, and rests in Christ's embrace, joyfully saying, "His left hand is under my head, and his right hand embraces me!" (Song 2:6).

Discussion Questions

 This chapter begins with Aelred being very busy taking care of the administrative tasks required of him as a Christian leader (2.1). What are the things today that keep Christian leaders "too busy" for true Christian friendships?

 In 2.14–15, Aelred and Walter discuss the idea that spiritual friendship is the best spiritual discipline for growing into spiritual maturity. Spiritual friendship is called the "best path" to becoming conformed to the image of Christ (2.15). To what extent do you agree with their claim? Would you want to qualify or even contradict this claim about the importance of spiritual friendship for growing into spiritual maturity?

 How do you feel about Aelred using three kinds of kisses to explain three different levels of friendship? Is his comparison of the abuse of a kiss to the abuse of "water, fire, iron, food, and air" helpful (2.25)? What kinds of signs of physical affection between two spiritual friends do you think are appropriate? In your culture, what kinds of signs of physical affection are deemed appropriate between friends of the same sex? What about between friends of the opposite sex?

At the start of this chapter (2.1), Aelred shows that he has developed the skill of being attentive to his friends. He is also able to ask them about potential negative emotions. What does this kind of attentiveness and honesty look like in your context today? What habits of observation and conversation are necessary for it to flourish?

Aelred wrote down notes about his conversation on friendship with Ivo (2.6). Gratian calls his conversation with Aelred about friendship a "feast" (2.17). Aelred was intentional and reflective about his friendships. What might it look like to be reflective about the friendships in your life? Would it look more like journaling ("taking notes") or like meeting with friends to talk? Do you do either of these on a regular basis? If not these activities, what other rhythms help you reflect about your friendships?

CHRISTIAN MINISTRY

Chapter 4

The Advantages and Excellence of Spiritual Friendship (Book 2.28–72)

Chapter Summary

If your friend decides to do something sinful, should you support them or challenge them? In this chapter we will find Aelred's answer to this and many other questions. When the last chapter concluded, Aelred had been explaining the nature of spiritual friendship using the example of three kinds of kisses. In this chapter, Aelred continues the conversation by answering a question from Walter about how far one should go for friendship (2.29–32). Aelred explains that true friends are willing to die for one another (2.33–36), and he explains that we do not have to be perfect to start on the journey of spiritual friendship (2.37–44). Pursuing true friendship is costly, however, and we should not be afraid to suffer for friendship because the pain is worth the gain (2.45–53).

Walter and Gratian agree that spiritual friendship is valuable, but they wonder how to distinguish spiritual friendships from lesser versions of friendship (2.54–56). Aelred then describes "childish friendships" (2.57–59) and "business" or transactional friendships (2.60–63). Both kinds of lesser friendship fall short of spiritual friendship, which Aelred describes as friendship "completely centered upon God" (2.61). This second conversation concludes with a summary (2.64–69) and then previews the topics to be discussed in the final conversation (2.70–72).

Text

Gratian Begins to Understand the Difference between Fleshly Friendship and Spiritual Friendship (2.28)

28. GRATIAN: I can see that friendship of this type is not common, nor are we accustomed even to dream of it being as you describe it. I do not know what Walter here has thought up to this point, but I always believed friendship to be nothing other than the identity of wills between two people, such that the one wishes nothing which the other does not wish; but so great is the agreement between the two on matters of good and evil that neither spirit, nor social status, nor honor, nor anything else that belongs to the one is denied to the other for his enjoyment and use, as he wishes.[1]

How Far Is "Too Far": The Limits of a Friendship? (2.29–32)

29. WALTER: I remember that I learned quite otherwise in the earlier dialogue, where the very definition of friendship was proposed and explained; it was this definition that

---

1   Gratian is describing the "fleshly friendship." See Aelred's description in *Spiritual Friendship*, 1.40.

rightly spurred me on to examine the fruits of friendship more closely. Since we have been sufficiently taught on this point, we are seeking to set up for ourselves a sure goal for this inquiry, the question of how far friendship ought to progress, since different people hold different opinions on this matter. For there are some who believe that a friend must be favored above faith, above honesty, above the public and private good; others believe that only faith should be removed from this list, and that, compared to friendship, the other matters are not to be worried over.

30. Still others believe that, for the sake of a friend, one should spurn money, eschew honors, endure the enmity of those in high places; they even believe that one should not avoid exile for the sake of a friend, and in matters in which one's homeland is not opposed or in which another person is not wrongly harmed, they believe that they must support a friend even in disgraceful and shameful circumstances. Also, there are those who establish this goal for friendship, that each person act with regard to a friend as he would act with regard to himself.[2]

31. Some people believe that they satisfy the demands of friendship if they repay a friend in turn for every benefit or favor rendered by the friend. But as for me, I am persuaded by our discussion that none of these limits must be granted. So I desire from you some indication of a sure goal for friendship, especially because of Gratian here, lest by chance

---

2   This last goal could be called "the golden rule": "Do unto others as you would have them do unto you" (Matt 7:12). Other versions of this basic rule of friendship can be found in Lev 19:34; Luke 6:31; 10:25–28; Gal 5:14; and Rom 13:9. See also versions in the Apocrypha like Tob 4:15 and Sir 31:15.

he prove true to his name and wish to be so gracious that he inadvertently become "vicious."[3]

32. GRATIAN: I can hardly be ungrateful for your concern for me; however, if my desire for listening did not hinder me, I would perhaps return the "favor" to you right now! But instead of that, let us both hear what response he wishes to make to your questions.

Spiritual Friends Are Willing to Die for One Another (2.33–36)

33. AELRED: Christ himself has set up a sure goal for friendship by saying, "Greater love has no one than this, that someone lay down his life for his friends" (John 15:13). Behold, how far love must be extended among friends— to the point that they are willing to die for one another! Does this satisfy you?

34. GRATIAN: Since there can be no greater love than this, why shouldn't this definition satisfy us?

35. WALTER: But what if some of the wicked or Gentiles so love one another in their agreement on crimes and shameful deeds that they are willing to die for one another—are we to agree that they have attained the pinnacle of friendship?

36. AELRED: By no means, since friendship cannot exist among the wicked.

---

3   Walter is teasing Gratian and making a joke using his name, but the pun does not really transfer into English.

What Kind of People Must We Be to Begin, Develop, and Perfect Spiritual Friendships? (2.37–41)

37. GRATIAN: Then describe, please, the sorts of people among whom friendship can arise or be preserved.

38. AELRED: I will describe it briefly. Friendship can arise among the good, it can progress among the better, but it can reach its highest point only among the best. For as long as a person intentionally delights in evil, as long as he prefers the dishonorable to what is honorable, as long as pleasure is more pleasing to him than purity, and boldness than moderation, and praise than modesty, how is it right for him even to aspire to friendship, since the beginning of friendship proceeds from the belief that one is virtuous? It is therefore difficult, if not impossible, for you to sample even the beginnings of friendship if you are ignorant of the source from which it arises.

> "Friendship can arise among the good, it can progress among the better, but it can reach its highest point only among the best."

39. For love is shameful and unworthy of the name of friendship, if in its name we demand something shameful of a friend; and this we force him to do, when he is either led or compelled to do evils of any kind whatsoever, when his own vices are neither laid to rest nor overcome. And so we ought to despise the opinion of those who believe that anything contrary to faith and honesty ought to be done on behalf of a friend.

40. For there is no excuse for sin, if you sin for the sake of a friend. The first man, Adam, would more safely have convicted his wife of presumption instead of taking the forbidden fruit by complying with her demand (*Gen* 3:6).

Indeed the servants of King Saul, by going against his command and keeping their hands from shedding blood, preserved their faith to him far better than Doeg the Edomite did, who, by acting as an agent of the king's cruelty, slew with his impious hands the priests of the Lord (*1 Sam 22:17–18*). And then there is Jonadab, the friend of Ammon, who should have kept his friend from incest and thereby acted more laudably than he would have by offering advice to enable his friend to attain his desired end (*2 Sam 13:3–5*).

41. Also, the virtue of friendship cannot excuse the friends of Absalom, who by giving assent to his treachery, took up arms against their country (*2 Sam 15:12*). And, to draw an example from our own day, it is certain that Otto, a cardinal of the Roman church, withdrew from his friend Guido far more happily than John stuck to his friend in the midst of such a great schism.[4] You can see, therefore, that friendship is not able to endure except among the "good."[5]

Are You Saying Only Perfect People Can Have Spiritual Friends? Is There Any Hope for Us? (2.42–44)

42. WALTER: So what has friendship to do with us, since we are not "good"?

---

4 This "current" example Aelred provides took place around 1159–1164. Can you think of a current example of friends who supported a high-profile Christian leader, despite that leader's significant ongoing sin, and somehow rationalized going along with their friend anyway?

5 Cicero, *On Friendship*, 5.18, 18.65.

43. AELRED: I do not define the "good" so closely—or, as Cicero said, "I do not go into that too deeply"—like those who maintain that no one is good except that person who lacks nothing in perfection.[6] We say that a good person is the one who, according to the way of our mortal flesh, lives a "self-controlled, upright, and godly [life] in the present age" (Titus 2:12), and desires to seek nothing dishonorable from anyone at all, nor to perform a dishonorable deed when asked. Indeed, we do not doubt that among such people friendships arise, by such people it is preserved, and in such people it is perfected.

44. And those who place themselves at the disposal of their friends' whims, even excepting either faith, or danger to their homeland, or unjust harm to another person—I would call these people not so much fools as insane: although they spare others, they do not spare themselves, and although they look out for the reputations of others, they unfortunately betray their own reputations.

Spiritual Friendship Is Costly and Some Are Not Willing to Pay the Price (2.45–48).

45. WALTER: I am just about to adopt the opinion of those Stoics who say that friendship should be avoided, that it is a thing full of cares and concerns, certainly not lacking in fear, and liable also to many griefs. For they say that, since it should be enough and more for each person to care for his own affairs, one is careless to obligate himself to others in such a way that he must be involved in many cares and be afflicted with many bothersome matters.

---

6   Ibid., 5.18.

46. Moreover they believe that nothing is "harder than for a friendship to continue to the very end of life," and that it would be exceedingly shameful, after a friendship has been initiated for that friendship to be turned into its opposite.[7] For these reasons they think it safer to love someone so as to be able to despise the person if one wishes; thus "the reins of friendship ought to be loosely held, so that one can tighten or loosen them as one wants."[8]

47. GRATIAN: But if we have so easily become indifferent to the natural appetite for friendship, we have all labored in vain—you in speaking and we in listening. You have commended friendship to us in so many ways as a thing whose fruit is so useful, so holy, so acceptable to God, so close to perfection.

Let those people have their opinion—those who are happy to love today so that they can hate tomorrow, or to be friends to all such that they need to be faithful to none; let them praise today and disparage tomorrow, flatter today and attack tomorrow, be ready for kisses today but hasten to blame tomorrow. The love of such people costs very little, and at the smallest offense it fades away.

48. WALTER: And I used to think that doves had no guts![vii] But tell us how these opinions, which have so displeased Gratian, can be refuted.

7　Ibid., 10.33.

8　Ibid., 13.45. This view could be summed up as, "the best way to the care-free life is simply not to care."

The Great Joy of Spiritual Friendship Requires Suffering (2.49)

49. AELRED: Cicero spoke well about such opinions of friendship: "They seem to take the sun out of the universe when they deprive life of friendship, because we have received nothing better, nothing more pleasant" from God than friendship.[9] What sort of wisdom is it to hate friendship so that you may avoid anxiety, leave cares behind, throw off fear—as though any virtue can be acquired or maintained without anxiety? And even in your own case, does prudence do battle with error, or temperance with desire, or justice with malice, or courage with cowardice, without causing you a great deal of trouble?

The Examples of the Apostle Paul and of David's Friend, Hushai (2.50–53)

50. Who, I wonder, especially among teenagers, is strong enough to protect his sexual purity, or to rein in his lusting affections, without the greatest concern and fear?[viii] Paul must have been a fool then, since he did not wish to live without care and concern for others, but rather with a view of Christian love, which he considered the greatest virtue, he was weak with the weak and he burned with desire along with those who were tempted (*2 Cor 11:28–29*). But he had great sadness and continual grief in his heart for his brothers according to the flesh (*Rom 9:2–3*).

51. Therefore he should have abandoned his Christian love, so he would not have to live under the burden of so many fears and griefs: now bringing to birth a second

---

9   Ibid., 13.47.

time those whom he had already begotten (*Gal 4:19*), nourishing his brethren like a nurse (*1 Thess 2:7*), now correcting them like a teacher (*2 Tim 2:25; Col 1:28*), now fearing lest their senses be corrupted (*2 Cor 11:3*), now with much pain and many tears calling them to repentance (*2 Cor 2:4*), now mourning those who did not show repentance (*2 Cor 12:21*). Do you see how those who dare to eliminate such anxieties, which always accompany virtue, do not fear to remove the virtues from the world?[ix]

52. Did Hushai the Arkite act foolishly when he so faithfully maintained that friendship which he had with King David, that he preferred trouble to security, and would rather share the griefs of a friend than to take his ease among the joys and honors of a parricide (*2 Sam 16:16–19; 17:5–16*)?

I would say that these are not so much humans as beasts who say that one ought to live so as to be a consolation to no one, to be a burden or a grief to no one, who derive no enjoyment from another person's good, who would cause through their own misfortune no bitterness at all to another person, but take care to love no one, and to be loved by no one.

> "I would say that these are not so much humans as beasts who... take care to love no one, and to be loved by no one."

53. Far be it from me, then, to grant that any of these people really loves, if they think that friendship is something to be bought. The benefit such people confer upon their "friends" is mere lip service, because they are either hoping for some temporal benefit, or trying to make their friends their helpers in some shameful deed.

How Do We Distinguish between Lesser Friendships and Spiritual Friendship? (2.54–56)

54. WALTER: Therefore, since it is certain that many are deceived by the appearance of friendship, please explain what sort of friendships we should avoid, and what sort we should seek out, nourish, and preserve.

55. AELRED: Since it has been agreed that friendship cannot exist except among the good, it is easy to see that you should accept no friendship which would disgrace people of good character.

56. GRATIAN: But perhaps we cannot discern clearly in making the distinction between what is disgraceful and what is not.

"Childish Friendship" Is Not Spiritual Friendship (2.57–59)

57. AELRED: I will do what you ask and briefly note the sorts of friendship I think should be avoided, when we encounter them.

There is childish friendship, the sort that comes from a wandering and sportive affection.[x] It follows every passerby (*Ezek 16:25*), without reason, without weight, without moderation, without any consideration of whether the friendship will be spiritually beneficial or not. This sort of friendship has a powerful effect for a while; it draws two people fairly close together, it beckons them flatteringly.

But affection without reason is the sort of attraction mere beasts feel for each other; among humans it is given to forming attachments that are in many respects illicit— indeed, it cannot tell the difference between the licit and the illicit. However, we understand that often affection precedes friendship, but it ought never to be followed unless it is led by reason, moderated by a sense of honor, and ruled by justice.

58. And so that sort of friendship, which I have characterized as childish simply because such affection holds sway more commonly among the young, should by all means be avoided by those who take delight in spiritual friendship, since it is unfaithful, unstable, and always alloyed with impure emotions.

I do not call it "friendship" so much as the "poison of friendship" since in it one is never able to maintain the legitimate expressions of love, which proceeds from one soul to another. Rather, arising like smoke from the lust of the flesh, it conceals and corrupts the honorable, natural quality of friendship until, with the neglect of the spirit, it leads to the desires of the flesh.

59. Therefore the beginning of spiritual friendship should be marked, first, by purity of intent, the advice of reason, and the guide of temperance; and so, if friendship is guided by these principles, when one experiences intense affection, this proper friendship will immediately appear pleasant, so that it never ceases to be well ordered.

(There is also the sort of friendship which is founded upon a similarity between shameful characters; but of this I will refuse to speak, since it is considered unworthy of the name of friendship, as we have said already.)[10]

---

10 See Aelred's discussion of "fleshy friendship" (1.38–41) and "worldly friendship" (1.42–44) above.

"Business Friendships" Are Not the Same as Spiritual Friendship (2.60–63)

60. There is also the friendship which is begun with a thought to some practical usefulness, which many people think a proper reason for a friendship to be sought, nourished and preserved. But if we grant this, how many of the most worthy people do we exclude from love of every sort! I mean those who own nothing, who have no possessions; those who think that friendship should have some practical benefit will not be able either to gain or to hope for some temporal benefit from those who are impoverished.

61. If indeed you would classify advice in doubt, consolation in adversity, and other things of this sort as "practical benefits," these things also are to be expected from a friend, but they ought to follow friendship, rather than precede it. For one who seeks from friendship some profit other than friendship itself has not yet learned what friendship is.

Friendship will be full of riches for those who cherish it when it is completely centered upon God; for those whom friendship joins together, it immerses in the contemplation of God.[11]

62. For although a faithful friendship between good people produces "many great benefits," I have no doubt that the benefits come from the friendship, rather than

---

11 Contemplation – "the core of the Christian life . . . the human counterpart to God's self-giving grace that is an openness to God's work in the Spirit, binding us to the life of Christ, that forms our fundamental posture of presenting ourselves to God." John Coe and Kyle Strobel, eds., *Embracing Contemplation: Reclaiming a Christian Spiritual Practice* (Downers Grove, IL: IVP Academic, 2019), 9.

vice versa.[12] I do not believe that the friendship of those two great men, David and Barzillai the Gileadite, owed its existence to the favors that Barzillai did when he received and supported David, and counted him as a friend, when he was fleeing his murderous son; instead, I do not doubt that such great favor came from friendship itself. For there is no one who believes that the king had any need of anything belonging to Barzillai before (2 Sam 17:27–29).

63. However, it is obvious that Barzillai, himself a man of great wealth, hoped for no gain in return for his kindness to the king, for when David eagerly offered him all the delights and riches of the state, he agreed to receive nothing, since he preferred to be content with what he already had (2 Sam 19:31–39).

So also that old covenant between David and Jonathan was consecrated not by hope of future benefit but by a vision of virtue; we know that it conferred much good on each, since the efforts of the one saved the life of the other—and it was as though Jonathan did himself a favor, since thereby his posterity was not destroyed (1 Sam 19–20; 2 Sam 9:1–13).

Summary of the Second Conversation (2.64–69)

64. Therefore, because among good people friendship always precedes and benefit follows, it is certainly the case that "benefits are not so much obtained through a friend as the love of a friend is itself a delight."[13]

---

12 Cicero, On Friendship, 9.30.

13 Ibid., 14.51.

And so you must now judge whether I have said enough about the fruit of friendship; or whether I have clearly distinguished those people, among whom friendship can certainly arise and be preserved and be perfected; or whether in addition I have showed palpably those sure goals toward which the love of friends ought to be directed.

65. WALTER: I do not remember that this last matter has been sufficiently explained.

66. AELRED: You recall, I think, that I have refuted the opinion of those who set up the goals of friendship in an agreement on vices and crimes; I have also refuted those who think that for the sake of a friend one ought even to go into exile, or to do any shameful deed whatever, provided that no harm is done to another.

67. I have also refuted those who measure the degree of friendship according to a standard of expected practical benefit. For I did not think it worth discussing the two opinions Walter mentioned, since what can be more inappropriate than to believe that friendship is extended only as far as repaying one's friend in turn through duties and kind words, when all things ought to be in common between those who surely ought to share "one heart and soul" (Acts 4:32)?

How shameful is this also, to feel no differently about a friend from how one feels about oneself, for each person ought to feel humility with regard to himself, and exaltation with regard to his friend.

68. Therefore, after dismissing these false goals of friendship, I maintained that the goal of friendship

ought to be derived from the words of the Lord, who ordained that even death itself should not be avoided on behalf of friends.

However, lest we have to agree that some shameful individuals, who so esteem each other that they are willing to die for each other, have reached the pinnacle of friendship, I explained that sort of persons among whom friendship is able to arise and be perfected. After that, we came to the opinion that those who believe friendship should be avoided because of its many concerns and cares must be convicted of folly. Finally, we unraveled—as briefly as we could—the question of what sorts of friendships ought to be avoided by good people generally.

69. And so from this we can see the certain and true goal of spiritual friendship: that is, nothing should be denied to a friend, and anything should be undertaken for a friend, even to the point at which we must lay down our life for our friend—a sacrifice ordained by divine authority (*John 15:13*).

Therefore, since the life of the soul is far more important than the life of the body, I believe that only this one thing should be denied to a friend: that which causes the death of the soul, which is nothing other than sin—that which separates God from the soul and the soul from life. But in these matters the questions of what favors should be showed to a friend, what should be endured for a friend, what mode of friendship ought to be preserved, what care observed in friendship—we do not have the time to settle now.

A Preview of the Third Conversation on Spiritual Friendship (2.70–72)

70. GRATIAN: I confess that my friend Walter has done me no small favor, since he has prodded you with his questions into giving a summary—a sort of brief epilogue—of all the matters we've discussed; it is as though you have vividly depicted our conversation before the eyes of memory itself. And now, please set forth for us the duties of friends, what moderation should be observed or what precautions taken.[xi]

71. AELRED: Both these and other matters concerning friendship remain to be dealt with. But our hour is gone, and those who just now came in, as you can see, are forcing me to other business with their brusqueness.

72. WALTER: I'm unwilling to yield to them—that's sure—but tomorrow I will certainly return when the opportunity presents itself. And let Gratian see to it that he be present tomorrow, lest he accuse us of negligence, and we accuse him of tardiness.

Discussion Questions

 In 2.40–41 Aelred explains that someone who supports their friend in sin is not a true friend. Aelred provides biblical examples as well as one from his own time. Can you think of current examples of friends who rationalized supporting a Christian leader despite significant ongoing sin? Would you have the courage to oppose a friend who is making a sinful choice?

 Aelred describes a "childish friendship" that is entered into "without reason, without weight, without moderation, without any consideration of whether the friendship will be spiritually beneficial or not" (2.57). Have you ever experienced a "childish friendship." How can we tell the difference between a childish friendship and a spiritual friendship (2.57–59)?

 Aelred states that prioritizing spiritual friendship is costly (2.45–49). He points to the Apostle Paul and to King David's friend, Hushai the Arkite, as examples of friends who suffered because of their commitment to true friendship (2.50–53). How do you feel about paying the price spiritual friendship requires? Is it an easy or difficult price to pay? In your experience, has the pain been worth the gain?

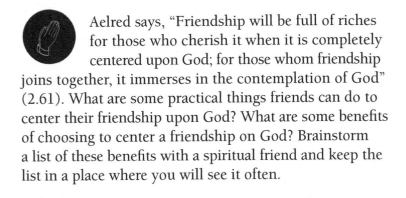 Aelred says, "Friendship will be full of riches for those who cherish it when it is completely centered upon God; for those whom friendship joins together, it immerses in the contemplation of God" (2.61). What are some practical things friends can do to center their friendship upon God? What are some benefits of choosing to center a friendship on God? Brainstorm a list of these benefits with a spiritual friend and keep the list in a place where you will see it often.

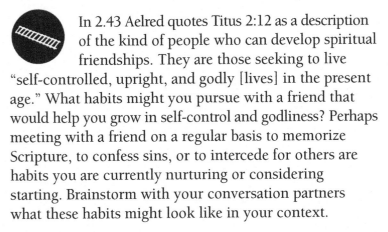 In 2.43 Aelred quotes Titus 2:12 as a description of the kind of people who can develop spiritual friendships. They are those seeking to live "self-controlled, upright, and godly [lives] in the present age." What habits might you pursue with a friend that would help you grow in self-control and godliness? Perhaps meeting with a friend on a regular basis to memorize Scripture, to confess sins, or to intercede for others are habits you are currently nurturing or considering starting. Brainstorm with your conversation partners what these habits might look like in your context.

CHRISTIAN MINISTRY

Chapter 5

Choosing Spiritual Friends
(Book 3.1–38)

Chapter Summary

Do you think a Christian leader should be very careful and intentional about choosing a spiritual friend? In this third, longest, and most practical instruction on spiritual friendship (Book 3), we find Aelred's answer to this pressing question. Aelred's conversation with Walter and Gratian is direct, personal, and practical. He begins by restating the difference between love and spiritual friendship. Christians are called to love everyone, but they can only be spiritual friends with a few (3.2–4). He emphasizes again that the only foundation for spiritual friendship is the mutual love of God (3.5–7).

Aelred then introduces a practical outline of how to develop spiritual friendships with four wise steps: (1) choosing, (2) testing, (3) accepting, and (4) enjoying friends (3.8–13). The first step is "choosing a spiritual friend," and the rest of Chapter 5 discusses "how to choose a friend" (3.14–38). Aelred is asked to explain his choice of two friends known to be a bit explosive, and his response shows that our spiritual friends do not need to be perfect (3.16–21, 31–38). Aelred warns about five habits that will destroy any friendship, and those displaying these characteristics should not be chosen as spiritual friends (3.21–27).

Text

Introduction to the Third Conversation (3.1)

1. AELRED: Where have you come from, and why are you here?

GRATIAN: Surely you have not forgotten the reason for my coming.

AELRED: But is Walter coming?

GRATIAN: Let him see to that himself. Certainly he will not be able to charge us with tardiness today.

AELRED: Do you want to follow up on those topics that we agreed on?

GRATIAN: I will trust Walter with that question. For I think I want him here for this conversation, since his mind is sharper than mine at understanding these things, and he has a better way of putting questions, and his memory is better at keeping a grasp on the matters we raise.

[Enter Walter.]

AELRED: Did you hear that, Walter? Gratian is more of a friend to you than you had supposed.

WALTER: How could he not be a friend to me, since he denies no one his friendship? But since we are now both here, let us not be ungrateful for this leisure, nor unmindful of your promise to converse further with us.

Love Does Not Require Friendship, but Friendship Requires Love (3.2–4)

2. AELRED: Love is the source and origin of friendship, for although love can exist without friendship, friendship can never exist without love. However, love can proceed either from nature, or from duty, or from reason alone, or from affection alone, or from each of these at the same time. An example of love proceeding from nature is the love of a mother for a child. Love proceeds from duty when we are joined together by some special affection that comes after love has been offered or received for a specific reason. Love from reason alone is exemplified by the love we have for enemies, which comes not from the spontaneous inclination of our minds to love our enemies, but from our obedience to a divine precept.

> *"Love is the source and origin of friendship, friendship can never exist without love."*

Love comes from affection alone when a person attracts the affection of others to himself simply because of physical qualities which we associate with the body, for example beauty, strength, or eloquence.

3. Love comes simultaneously from reason and affection when someone ingratiates himself in the mind of another through the attractiveness of his character and the delight one takes in his honorable life; the mind urges us to love this person simply because of the merit of his virtue. Thus reason is joined to affection, so that love is pure

because it comes from reason, and agreeable because it comes from affection. Which of these sources of love do you think is more suited for friendship?

4. WALTER: This last one, surely! It is both formed by the contemplation of virtue and adorned by the attraction of good character. But I would like to know whether all of those whom we come to love in this fashion should be admitted to the secret joys of our friendship.

Love for God Is the Foundation and Limit of Spiritual Friendship (3.5–7)

5. AELRED: One must first lay a solid foundation for spiritual friendship upon which its principles may be based. If this is done, the person who is ascending the higher reaches of spiritual love by a direct path ought not to neglect this foundation nor go beyond it, but instead exercise the greatest caution. The foundation of which I speak is the love of God; by this foundation we should measure all those things which either love or affection prompts, all those things which either the heart secretly suggests or some friend openly urges. We must be especially careful that whatever we add to this foundation fits with it, and whatever exceeds this foundation, you will agree, must be brought back in line with it and corrected in every way, according to the pattern of the foundation.

6. Nor must all of those whom we love be received into our friendship, since not everyone is worthy of it.

"For a friend is the sharer of your soul, to your friend's spirit you join and attach your own, and you so mingle the two that you would like for your two spirits to become one."[1]

You might say that "you entrust yourself to him as to another self"; you hide nothing from your friend, and "from your friend you fear nothing."[2]

Since this is so, you first choose someone whom you think to be conformable to these qualities, and then you test this person, and only then do you admit him to your friendship. "For friendship ought to be stable," and to offer a certain prospect of eternity, persevering in affection.[3]

7. So also "we ought not to change our friends in a childish manner, following some unsettled notion."[4] For since there is no more hateful person than he who offends against a friendship, and nothing torments the spirit more than to be deserted or attacked by a friend, a friend must therefore be chosen with the utmost zeal and tested with the greatest caution. However, once a friend has been accepted, he must be so tolerated, treated, and agreed with that, as long as he has not permanently departed from that foundation of friendship which we have agreed on, he will belong to you and you to him, as much in temporal as in spiritual matters, so that there will be no differences between you on affairs of the soul, the affections, your wills and opinions.

---

1 Ambrose, *On the Duties of the Clergy*, 3.134.

2 Ibid.

3 Ibid., 3.128.

4 Ibid.

Four Steps to Spiritual Friendship (3.8–13)

8. Therefore you can see the four steps by which we ascend to the perfection of friendship: the first is choice, the second is testing, the third is acceptance, and the fourth is "the highest agreement on both human and divine affairs, combined with good will and affection."[5]

Four Steps to Spiritual Friendship	
Choosing	3.14-58
Testing	3.59-75
Accepting	3.76
Enjoying	3.76-87

9. WALTER: I remember that you approved of this definition in the first discussion you had with your friend Ivo; but I wish to know whether this definition holds for everyone, since you have dealt with many different types of friendships.

10. AELRED: Since true friendship cannot exist except among good people—I mean those who can neither desire nor actually do anything contrary to faith or good morals—this definition embraces not every friendship whatsoever, but only that which is true friendship.

11. GRATIAN: Why should we not equally approve of that definition that pleased me so much before yesterday's

---

5 Cicero, *On Friendship*, 6.20.

conversation, namely, that friendship is an agreement to share the same likes and dislikes?[6]

12. AELRED: This definition is certainly valid among those whose characters have been corrected, whose lives are in order and whose affections are under control; I do not think it should be rejected by such people as these.

13. WALTER: Let Gratian see to it that these qualities you just mentioned are present both in himself and in the person whom he loves. In this way his friend will agree with him both about what he wants and about what he does not want: since he has not been asked to do anything which is either unjust or dishonorable or indecent, he will not ask that anything of the sort be done for him.

But we are waiting for you to tell us what we should think about those four steps of friendship you have already mentioned.

Step 1: How to Choose a Friend (3.14–15)

14. AELRED: Then let us deal first with the choice of a friend. There are certain vices which will not allow a person involved with them to preserve either the obligations or rights of friendship for very long. It is not easy to choose friends, for a friendship of the sort we are speaking about; but if their lives and habits are otherwise suitable, we should treat them in every way so that they may be corrected and thus considered worthy for friendship—I mean people who may be prone to anger, or flightiness, or those who may be distrustful or talkative.

---

6   See *Spiritual Friendship*, 1.35.

15. Indeed, it is difficult for one who often is stirred up with the fury of anger not to attack his friend from time to time, as it says in Ecclesiasticus: "There are friends who change into enemies, and tell of the quarrel to your disgrace" (Sir 6:9). So Scripture says: "Make no friendship with a man given to anger, nor go with a wrathful man, lest you learn his ways and entangle yourself in a snare" (Prov 22:24–25). And Solomon said, "Anger lodges in the bosom of fools" (Eccl 7:9). But who will not think it impossible to maintain a friendship with a fool for very long?

The Friends We Choose Do Not Have to Be Perfect (3.16–21)

16. WALTER: But, unless we are mistaken, we have seen that you have cultivated a friendship of the highest devotion with a man who was very prone to anger, a man to whom you never did any harm even to the end of his life, although—we have heard—he often harmed you.

17. AELRED: There are some who, through their natural constitution, are prone to anger, but who are so accustomed to control and moderate their passion that they never fall into those five sins which, as Scripture bears witness, can cause a friendship to dissolve (*Sir* 22:22). However, they may sometimes offend a friend by an inconsiderate word, or by an action, or by a zeal that is less than discrete. If by chance we have taken such people into our friendship, we must put up with them patiently; and since we have some certainty about their affection for us, if there is any excessive speech or action on their part, we must indulge it because they are our friends, or certainly we ought to admonish them, but do it without causing grief, or even do it pleasantly.

18. GRATIAN: We think that a friend of yours, whom you prefer to all of us (as it seems to many), a few days ago both did and said something which clearly displeased you—it was impossible to miss it—and yet we do not see any evidence that your prior good will toward him is at all diminished. And so we are quite mystified that, as we speak together, you make no demands upon him, or put up with the trifles that he asks of you, while he himself cannot abide any trifle for your sake.

19. WALTER: Gratian is far bolder than I. For I also know these things, but I did not presume to discuss any of these matters with you, since I am aware of your feelings for this man.

20. AELRED: Indeed that man is most dear to me, and at the same time, since I have received him in friendship, it will never be possible for me not to love him. And so if by chance I was stronger in this matter than he was, and since our two wills did not agree on the matter, it was easier for me to give up my desire than it was for him. Where there was no question of dishonesty, where no harm came to faith and virtue was not diminished, I had to yield to my friend, so that I might put up with him where he appeared to transgress, and where his peace was endangered, I might put his will before my own.

Five Habits That Will Destroy Any Friendship (3.21–27)

21. WALTER: But although your earlier friend has now gone on to his reward, your other friend—this was impossible for us to overlook—has pleased you. But now I would have you lay out for us those five reasons by which friendship is so harmed that it is dissolved, so that

we ourselves may avoid those persons who ought never to be taken into our circle of friends.

22. AELRED: Don't listen to me, but hear the voice of Scripture: "One who reviles a friend destroys a friendship. Even if you draw your sword against a friend, do not despair, for there is a way back. If you open your mouth against your friend, do not worry, for reconciliation is possible" (Sir 22:20–22). Consider what the Scripture is saying. If by chance your friend is overcome by anger and draws his sword, or if he grieves you by something he says, or if he withdraws himself from you for a time as though he no longer loves you, or if he sometimes prefers his own counsel to yours, or if he disagrees with you on some idea or dispute, you should not think that your friendship should be ended just because of these things.

> **Five Habits That Destroy Friendship**
>
> (1) Slander (23)
>
> (2) Reviling a Friend (24)
>
> (3) Arrogance (24)
>
> (4) Betraying Secrets (24-25)
>
> (5) Backstabbing (25)

23. "For there is reconciliation with a friend," as Scripture says, "with the exception of slander, impropriety, pride, the betrayal of confidences, and backstabbing. In all these instances, a friend will flee." (Sir 22:22).[7] Therefore, we should consider these five reasons, lest we bind ourselves with the fetters of friendship to those who fall prey to these vices either by the fury of anger or some other passion.

---

7   Protestant Christians would not agree with Aelred that Sirach is Scripture, but rather would call it a spiritual classic. Aelred appears to be reading from a variant reading of Sirach 22:22. Modern translations of Sirach 22:22 list four, not five, reasons for breaking off a friendship: "But as for reviling, arrogance, disclosure of secrets, or a treacherous blow—in these cases any friend will take to flight."

Because slander does harm to a person's reputation, it extinguishes the flame of Christian love. For the malice of humankind is so great that, whatever one friend blurts out against another under in a fit of anger, even if it is not believed, is passed around as though it came from the confidant of his deepest secrets.[xii]

24. For many people delight as much in reviling others as they do in receiving praise themselves. But what is more criminal than slander that fills the face of its innocent victim with pitiable blushing over its false accusation? Or what is less to be tolerated than the sort of arrogance that excludes the remedy of humble confession, which alone can restore a broken friendship? It is arrogance that makes a person bold to commit the injury in the first place, and then too haughty to accept correction.

Then there is the betrayal of a friend's innermost secrets; nothing is more shameful than this, or more abominable, since it leaves no room for love, or favor, or pleasure between friends, but fills all their relationship with bitterness and sours it with the gall of indignation, hatred and pain.

25. Hence it is written, "Whoever betrays secrets destroys confidence" (Sir 27:16). And a little later, "Whoever has betrayed secrets is without hope" (Sir 27:21). For who is more miserable than the one who destroys trust and grows weak to the point of hopelessness?

And finally, there is backstabbing, the last fault which dissolves friendship, which is nothing other than secret character assassination.[xiii] Indeed, it is a deceitful blow, like the fatal blow delivered by a viper or asp: "If the serpent bites before it is charmed," says Solomon, "there is no advantage to the charmer" (Eccl 10:11).

26. Therefore you should avoid anyone whom you find
to be beset by these vices, and you shouldn't choose such
a one for friendship until he is restored to moral health.
Let us therefore renounce insults—God is their avenger.
When the holy man David was fleeing before his son
Absalom, Shimei attacked him with insults; but later,
when David lay dying and he gave to his son his last
instructions, he deemed Shimei worthy to be killed,
according to the authority of the Holy Spirit (*1 Kings
2:8–9; 2 Sam 16:3–13*). No less ought we to avoid
reproaching others. The hapless Nabal of Carmel deserved
to be struck down by the Lord and die, because he
reproached David for servitude and for fleeing from
Absalom (*1 Sam 25:10–38*). But if by chance it happens
that we should neglect the law of friendship with respect
to some friend, let us shun pride and seek to win back our
friend's favor by a deed done in humility.

27. When King David offered to Hanun, the son of
Nahash king of the Ammonites, the same friendship
he had offered to his father, the proud and ungrateful
Hanun added insult to his contempt for his father's friend
(*1 Chron 19:1–20:1; 2 Sam 10:1–4; 12:26–31*). For this
reason, both fire and sword consumed his people and his
cities. However, we should think it a sacrilege above
all others to betray the confidences of friends, for which
reason trust is lost and despair is brought home upon
the captive soul. So it is that the impious Ahithophel went
along with the would-be parricide Absalom; but when
he had betrayed to Absalom his father's strategy, and then
saw that the plan he had himself suggested against
David's was not accepted, he hanged himself—a death
he richly deserved as a traitor (*2 Sam 16:15–17:23*).

Other Characteristics to Avoid
When Looking for a Friend (3.28–30)

28. Finally, let us consider it a poison to friendship to slander a friend, the deed which caused Miriam's face to break out with leprosy, and caused her to be cast out of the camp and deprived of fellowship with her people for six days (*Num 12:1–15*).

Not only ought we to avoid choosing as friends those who are prone to excessive anger, but also those who are flighty and suspicious as well. For since the great fruit of friendship is the confidence with which you may believe your friend and entrust yourself to him, how can you have any confidence at all in one who is blown about by every breeze, or who gives his assent to each and every plan? Such a man's affections are like soft clay, receiving and forming different and contradictory images all day long, according to the will of the one making the impression at the time.

29. Moreover, what is more fitting to friendship than that mutual peace and tranquility of heart which a suspicious man never knows, because he can never rest? For inquisitiveness always accompanies the suspicious man, goading him constantly and sharply, and supplying him with the sources of restlessness and worry. Thus, whenever he sees his friend speaking rather confidentially with someone else, he will immediately suspect that he is being betrayed. And if the suspicious man's friend shows himself to be well-disposed toward another, or pleasant, he will immediately complain that his friend esteems him less. If he is ever corrected by his friend, he will take the correction as a sign of dislike; even if his friend thinks

that the suspicious man is to be complimented, he complains that his friend is really making fun of him.

30. Also, I do not think that a talkative person ought to be chosen as a friend, because "should . . . a man full of talk be judged right?" (Job 11:2). The Wise Man says, "Do you see a man who is hasty in his words? There is more hope for a fool than for he" (Prov 29:20).

Therefore this is the sort of man you should choose for a friend: one who is not troubled by the fury of anger, nor divided against himself by instability; one whom suspicion does not wear out, nor talkativeness loose from the dignity that is customary among us.[xiv] It will be especially useful if you choose as a friend one whose character and nature fit your own. As the blessed Ambrose said, "Friendship cannot exist between those who are quite different in character, and so there needs to be a similar measure of goodwill on both sides."[8]

Aelred's Spiritual Friends Are Not Perfect (3.31–38)

31. WALTER: Where then can such a person be found, who is neither prone to anger, not unstable, nor given to suspicion? (For I'll grant you that whoever is too talkative cannot hide his vice.)

32. AELRED: I agree that it is difficult to find a friend who is not very often moved by these passions, but there are surely many who can be found to be superior to all of these. They are the sort who suppress anger with patience, who restrain flightiness by maintaining their dignity, who rid themselves of their suspicions by contemplating love. I should say that these most of all should be taken into

---

8   Ambrose, *On the Duties of the Clergy*, 3.133.

Ambrose and His Friend Augustine

friendship as they are more practiced in overcoming vices through virtue—I mean those who can be held by the bond of friendship more securely since they are accustomed to resist the temptations of vice more bravely.

33. WALTER: Please don't be angry with me for saying this, but that friend of yours of whom Gratian spoke a short while ago: We do not doubt that you received him into friendship, but I wish to know whether he ever seems prone to anger to you.[9]

34. AELRED: He does indeed, but not at all in our friendship.

35. GRATIAN: What do you mean, that he is not prone to anger in friendship?

36. AELRED: You do not doubt that there is a bond of close friendship between us?

GRATIAN: Not at all.

AELRED: When have you ever heard that anger, strife, disagreements, rivalries, or arguments arose between us?

GRATIAN: Never; but we thought that this was because of your patience, not his.

37. AELRED: You are wrong. For there is no way one friend's patience will rein in anger which the other's affection does not itself rein in; on the contrary, by a show of patience one often goads the irascible man into fury—for the sole purpose of gaining for oneself some bit of solace if the other shows himself to be his equal in angry disputes. Now, with regard to that man of whom

---

9 See *Spiritual Friendship*, 3.16–21.

we're now speaking, he so maintained the rights of friendship with me that when he was moved to utter angry words and, indeed, when he was already bursting forth into speech I could restrain him with only a nod of my head; he never publicly mentioned those matters which were the cause of his anger, but he always waited until we were alone to unburden his mind.

38. But if it were not his friendship for me that made him do this, but rather his nature that dictated it, I would not think him either so virtuous or so worthy of praise. And if, as indeed happens, my opinion differs from his from time to time, we defer to each other so that sometimes he submits to my will, but more often I submit to his.

Discussion Questions

Aelred states that the only foundation for a spiritual friendship is the love of God. He teaches that we need to continually return to this foundation and evaluate our own loves and relationships in light of this first love (3.5). As you think about the culture around you, what are the foundations used to build friendships?

We carefully choose the clothes we wear, the food we eat, the places we invest our money and time, do you agree with Aelred that we should also carefully choose our friends (3.14)?

How do you feel about Aelred's teaching that Christians are called to love all people, including their enemies, but they can only accept a limited number into their lives as spiritual friends (3.2)? Does this feel unfair to you? Does it make you feel relieved? Share with one another the kinds of emotions that arise as you consider Aelred's claim.

Aelred has learned about friendship from his historical mentor Ambrose (d. 397), who lived some seven hundred years earlier. Aelred quotes Ambrose's description of a friend as "the sharer of your soul," someone to whom "you entrust yourself to as to another self" and "from whom you fear nothing" (3.30). Elsewhere Aelred quotes Gregory the Great's definition of a friend as the "guardian of my soul." What practical advice from this chapter would help you become the kind of friend that Ambrose and Gregory describe?

 Aelred's thinking about spiritual friendship has been shaped by reading the spiritual classic Wisdom of Sirach. Aelred uses Sirach to warn about five habits that can destroy a friendship: (1) slander (3.23), (2) reviling (3.24), (3) arrogance (3.24), (4) betraying secrets (3.24–25), and (5) backstabbing (3.25).[10] Which of these habits is most likely to be a barrier keeping you from forming spiritual friendships?

---

10 To read more from Sirach about friendship, see Bob Lay, ed., *Books Jesus Read: Learning from the Apocrypha*, Sacred Roots Spiritual Classics 5 (Wichita, KS: The Urban Ministry Institute Press, 2022), 172–78.

CHRISTIAN MINISTRY

Chapter 6

Testing Spiritual Friends
(Book 3.39-75)

Chapter Summary

Are you comfortable testing your friends? If you were
going to test them, what would you test them on? This
sixth chapter provides Aelred's answers to these and
many more questions. In the last chapter, Aelred introduced
four steps to finding spiritual friends, and he discussed
the first step: choosing a spiritual friend. Now, in Chapter
6, the conversation continues with Walter asking what
to do if you discover that the friend you have chosen has
a serious character flaw; Aelred replies by providing a
number of practical suggestions (3.39–51). Aelred then
provides a helpful summary of the conversation so far
(3.52–58), before moving to the second step in finding
a spiritual friend: testing your friend's character (3.59–61).
Aelred identifies four characteristics to test in a potential
spiritual friend: (1) faithfulness (3.62–67), (2) intentions
(3.68–71), (3) good judgement (3.72), and (4) patience

(3.73). Finally, this chapter concludes with Aelred providing several additional principles for testing a potential spiritual friend (3.74–75).

Text

What Do You Do If You Discover Serious Character Flaws in a Spiritual Friend after You Have Already Chosen Them? (3.39–44)

39. WALTER: That explanation will satisfy Gratian. But I wish that you would explain to me what one should do if he has perhaps carelessly fallen into a friendship with those whom you just warned us to avoid; or, in the case of those whom you said we should choose as friends, what sort of faith should we keep with them, or what sort of favor should we show them, if they have pursued either those vices which you just mentioned or some other, worse vices?

40. AELRED: These sorts of problems should be avoided, if at all possible, in the act of choosing itself, or even in the process of testing potential friends, so that we may be sure not to form intimacies too quickly, particularly with those unworthy of such regard.[xv] "They are most worthy of friendship in whom there exists the reason why they should be loved."[1] Nevertheless, even in those who are thought tested and worthy of friendship, "vices often break forth, both against their own friends, and against strangers, whose shame nevertheless redounds to their friends."[2] We must make every effort to restrain such friends, so that they may be healed from their vices.

1　Cicero, *On Friendship*, 21.79.

2　Ibid.

41. But if this proves to be impossible, I do not think that the friendship should be immediately broken or surrendered, but rather, as someone in Cicero's dialogue cleverly says, a friendship "should be unstitched little by little, unless by chance some intolerable injury has come to light, such that it is neither right nor honorable for there not to be an immediate estrangement or parting of the ways."[3] For if a friend does something either against his father, or against his homeland, which cries out for immediate and hurried correction, the law of friendship is not harmed if he is given up as a traitor and an enemy.

42. But there are other vices for which friendship ought not to be broken, as I just said, but rather ought to be dissolved little by little, in my opinion. However, this ought to be done carefully so that it doesn't end up "in enmity, from which come disputes, curses and insults."[4] For it is excessively "shameful to carry on a dispute with someone" of this sort, "with whom you have lived very closely."[5]

43. For even if you are attacked for all these reasons by the one you have taken into friendship, it will be because it is the custom of some to cast the blame back upon their friends if they have themselves lived in such a way that they are no longer worthy to be loved; and if some adversity comes to them, they say that their friends have done harm to their friendship, and they hold in suspicion every counsel offered to them by their friends; and when they are revealed, and their crimes have come into the open, and they have nothing else to do, they redouble their

---

3   Ibid.
4   Ibid., 21.76.
5   Ibid., 21.77.

hatred and their curses against their friends, slandering them on the street corners and whispering against them in the alleys, falsely excusing themselves and in the same fashion blaming others.

44. Therefore, if you have ended the friendship and are afterwards attacked in all these ways, "as long as the attacks are bearable they should be borne; and this honor must be paid to a former friendship, that he who commits an injury is to blame, not he who suffers it."[6] For friendship is eternal, and so Scripture says, "A friend loves at all times" (Prov 17:17). If the person you love harms you, love him still. If he is such a person that you think your friendship with him should be withdrawn, still you should never withdraw your love for him. Be mindful, as far as you can, of his good; watch out for his reputation, and never betray the secrets of your friendship with him, even if he betrays yours.

Reasons to Stop a Spiritual Friendship and Examples from Scripture (3.45–52)

45. WALTER: Please tell us those faults for which you say a friendship should be gradually dissolved.

46. AELRED: They are the five faults I described a little while ago, especially the betrayal of confidences and the hidden stings of backstabbing. To these I add a sixth. There is the friend who offends those whom you feel equally obliged to love, and who, though corrected, does not cease to be a cause of ruin and stumbling to those whose well-being is your proper concern—especially when the disgrace of his misdeeds touches you. For love

---

6 Ibid., 21.78.

of a friend ought not to outweigh religion, or faithfulness, or love for one's fellow citizens, or the good of the people.

47. King Xerxes hanged that exceedingly proud man Haman on a cross, although he had considered him a friend above all others, because the king preferred the good of his people and the love of his wife to the friendship which Haman had damaged with his dishonest counsels (*Esth 7*). And although there were good relations between Sisera and the house of Heber, Jael, the wife of Heber the Kenite, killed Sisera with a hammer and nail because she believed that the safety of her people was more important than this friendship (*Judg 4:17–22*). According to the law of friendship the holy prophet David ought to have kept alive the relatives of Jonathan; but he heard from the Lord that the people had been beset by hunger continuously for three years on account of Saul and his bloody house, because they had killed the Gibeonites, and so he handed over to the Gibeonites seven of Saul's relatives to be punished (*2 Sam 21:1–9*).

48. However, I do not wish you to be unaware of the fact that there can be no rupture between those perfect friends who have been wisely chosen and carefully joined together in true spiritual friendship. When friendship has made two people one, just as that which is one cannot be divided, so also friendship cannot be separated from itself. Therefore, it is clear that friendship which suffers division was never true friendship in that respect in which it is damaged, since "friendship which can cease was never true friendship."[7]

---

7   Jerome, *Letters*, 3.6.

49. However, in this respect friendship is more praiseworthy and its virtue is more clearly proved, when a friend does not cease to be the friend he was, even to one who harms him: he loves the one by whom he is not loved, he honors the one by whom he is despised, he blesses the one by whom he is cursed, and he does good to the one who devises ruin for him (*Luke 6:28*).[xvi]

50. GRATIAN: How then is friendship dissolved if such kindnesses must be shown to the former friend by the one who dissolves the friendship?

51. AELRED: Four considerations seem to hold especially in the case of friendship: love, affection, security, and delight. Friendship involves love when there is a show of favor that proceeds from good will. It involves affection when a certain inner pleasure comes from friendship. It involves security when it leads to a revelation of all one's secrets and purposes without fear or suspicion. It involves delight when there is a certain meeting of the minds—an agreement that is pleasant and benevolent—concerning all matters, whether happy or sad, which have a bearing on the friendship, everything that we teach or learn.

> "Four considerations seem to hold especially in the case of friendship: love, affection, security, and delight."

52. Do you see how one must dissolve friendship with those who once deserved it? Indeed, that inner delight one continually drinks in as though straight from the heart of a friend is removed; that security in which one reveals one's secrets to a friend passes away; and the pleasure begotten by friendly conversation is set aside.

Finally, that familiarity which embraces these accessories to friendship must be denied him, but love must not be withdrawn. Moreover, this process of withdrawal should be performed with a certain moderation and reverence, such that unless there is excessive revulsion between the two former friends, some traces of the old friendship always appear to remain.

Aelred Summarizes His Main Points So Far (3.52–58)

53. GRATIAN: What you say is certainly very agreeable to me.

AELRED: Tell me whether what I've said about the choice of friends is sufficient.

WALTER: I would prefer that you give us a summary, sort of a brief epilogue, of the things that you said.

54. AELRED: I'll grant your request. I said that love is the beginning of friendship. Not love of every kind whatsoever, but that which proceeds at once from reason and affection, which is indeed chaste because it proceeds from reason, and agreeable because it proceeds from affection. Finally, I said that a foundation must be laid for friendship, namely, the love of God. To this love of God everything that has to do with friendship must be compared; one must examine whether the concerns of a friendship are in keeping with the love of God, or opposed to it.

> "To this love of God everything that has to do with friendship must be compared."

55. After that, I maintained that we should establish four steps by which one reaches the summit of friendship: first, a friend must be chosen; then he must be tested; then at length he must be admitted to our friendship; and

finally he must be treated as is fitting. In dealing with the choice of friends, we concluded that those who are prone to anger, unstable, suspicious, and talkative are ineligible for friendship—not all, however, but only those who are either incapable or unwilling to order or control these passions. For many are beset by these disturbing vices in such a way that not only is their perfection not harmed in any way, but their virtue in controlling these vices is quite laudably increased.

56. For those who are always carried about headlong by these passions, like unbroken horses, inevitably slip and fall into the vices which, as Scripture bears witness, both harm and dissolve friendship, that is, "disputes, the betrayal of secrets and other improper matters, pride, and backbiting" (Sir 22:22).[8]

57. Nevertheless, if you should suffer all these things from one whom you have taken into your friendship, I say that the friendship should not be immediately broken off, but rather dissolved little by little, and such reverence for the old friendship should be maintained as permits you to withdraw your inner secrets from your former friend. However, you should never withdraw your love from him, or refuse him aid, or deny him counsel. But if your former friend's madness breaks out into blasphemy and curses, you should still defer to the bond that linked you—defer to charity—so that the one who blasphemes or curses is to blame, not the one who suffers the injury.

58. On the other hand, if a man is found to be harmful to his family, his country, his fellow citizens, his underlings, or his friends, the bond of familiarity must be broken

---

8   See *Spiritual Friendship*, 3.21–27.

immediately; the love of one person must not outweigh the harm of many. Great caution must be taken in the choice of friends if such problems are to be avoided in the first place. That is, you should choose as a friend one who is not compelled to such deeds by anger, whom fickleness does not drag down, who is not sent reeling by talkativeness, nor led away by suspicion.[xvii] Most of all, you should not choose as a friend one whose character and habits are very different from your own, or whose nature clashes with yours.

Step 2: Test Your Friend on Four Character Qualities (3.59–61)

59. But because I am speaking about true friendship, which cannot exist except among the good, there cannot be any doubt about those of whom I have made no mention—the shameful, greedy, ambitious, or reproachful—that these should not be chosen for friendship. If you are satisfied with what I have said about choosing friends, let us move on next to the testing of friends.

WALTER: This is opportune, for I'm keeping my eye on the door, expecting someone to interrupt us and put an end to our pleasure, or inject a note of sadness, or make some meaningless remark.

[A sound from outside the room; Gratian goes to the door.]

60. GRATIAN: The steward is here; if we let him in, you won't be able to go on any further. Here, I will watch the door; you, Father, continue on where you began.

[Gratian sends the steward away, and rejoins the conversation.]

61. AELRED: Four qualities ought to be tested in a friend: faithfulness, intent, judgment, and patience. You should test your friend's faithfulness so that you may entrust yourself and all that you have to him. Test his intent, to ensure that he is looking for nothing from the friendship except God and that natural good that comes from your mutual friendship. Test his judgment, so that your friend not be ignorant of the obligations and demands of friendship, the matters in which friends must weep or rejoice together; and let him be aware both under what circumstances we believe friends must sometimes be corrected, and the proper means, time, and place for such correction. Finally, test your friend's patience, to make sure that he is not grieved by correction, and does not despise or hate the one who corrects him, but is willing to endure any adversity for the sake of his friend.

> *"Four qualities ought to be tested in a friend: faithfulness, intent, judgment, and patience."*

Testing a Friend's Faithfulness/Loyalty (3.62–67)

62. In friendship there is nothing more outstanding than faithfulness, which seems to be both the nurse and the guardian of friendship.[xviii] In all of life's turns, in adversity and prosperity, in joy and sadness, in delightful and bitter circumstances, it reveals itself to be comparable to friendship, holding in the same regard both the humble and the exalted, the poor and the rich, the strong and the weak, the well and the infirm. Thus the faithful man sees nothing in his friend that is alien to his own spirit; he honors virtue in its own proper place, but considers all other qualities external to his friend and does not test them much if he finds them present, nor seek them much if they are absent.

63. Still, this faithfulness is invisible when all is going well, but it comes to the fore in adversity. As someone has said, "It is when times are hard that a friend can be properly proved."[9] The wealthy man has many friends (*Prov 14:20*), but a sudden decline into poverty shows whether they are true friends. "A friend loves at all times," says Solomon, "and a brother is born for adversity" (Prov 17:17). And in another passage, blaming the faithless, he says, "Trusting in a treacherous man in time of trouble is like a bad tooth or a foot that slips" (Prov 25:19).

64. GRATIAN: But if no adversity ever alters our prosperity, how is a friend's faithfulness tested?

65. AELRED: There are many other ways to test a friend's faithfulness, although the best test is adversity. For as I said above, there is nothing which does more harm to friendship than betrayal of counsel. Indeed, this is the Gospel's thought: "One who is faithful in a very little is also faithful in much" (Luke 16:10; *19:17*). And so we ought not to entrust everything, and certainly not our deep secrets, to friends whom we think it still necessary to test; rather, we should entrust them with confidences that are small, not so deep, about which we need not exercise great caution, to see whether they keep these secrets or reveal them—but we should do this with as much care as would suggest that our friends would do us a grave disservice to reveal them, or a great favor to keep them.

66. If you find a friend who is faithful in these small matters, you should not hesitate to test him in more important things. But if by chance some unfavorable rumor about you spreads, or if someone maliciously attacks your

---

9 Ambrose, *On the Duties of the Clergy*, 3.130.

reputation, and your friend is not led by innuendo to give credence to these rumors, if he is not moved by suspicion or disturbed by any doubt, you should have no further hesitation about his faithfulness, but instead you should rejoice greatly over his sure and stable faithfulness.

67. GRATIAN: I'm thinking now of that friend of yours across the sea, whom you often mentioned to us as most tried and true, a very faithful friend, because he not only maintained his faithfulness when some were making false accusations against you, but he also was steadfast and unmoved by any doubt whatsoever—a thing you would not have thought to presume even of your best friend, the old sacristan of Clairvaux.[10] But since we have sufficiently covered the testing of a friend's faithfulness, please go on to explain the other matters.

The Test of a Friend's Intentions (3.68–71)

68. AELRED: I said also that one must test a friend's intent. This is quite essential, for there are very many who recognize nothing good in human affairs unless it leads to some temporal gain. Thus these people love their friends just as they love their herds of cattle—"from them they hope to get" something useful.[11] Indeed, they lack full spiritual friendship, which they ought to seek for its own sake—or rather, for God's sake and for its own sake; they do not contemplate the natural example of love in themselves, where its "strength and quality and magnitude" can be easily comprehended.[12]

---

10 Sacristan – a church officer who cares for the bread and wine for the Lord's Supper, oils, relics, church decorations, and other similar items.

11 Cicero, On Friendship, 21.79.

12 Ibid., 21.80.

69. Our Lord and Savior himself prescribed for us the form of true friendship when he said, "Love your neighbor as yourself" (Matt 22:39; *Lev 19:18*). Behold, here is the reflection of love: Do you love yourself? Yes, indeed, if you love God, and surely if you are the sort of person I described as worthy to be chosen for friendship. But do you think that you should give yourself some reward for this love of yourself? Not at all: everyone holds himself dear. Therefore, unless you transfer this affection for yourself to another, and love your friend freely, because your friend is dear to you simply because of who he is, you will not be able to enjoy the pleasures of true friendship.

70. For then the person you love will become like another self once you have taken your Christian love and poured it forth onto him.[xix] As the blessed Ambrose said, "Friendship does not exist to produce income, but rather is full of beauty and grace. Thus it is a virtue, not something to be acquired, because it is begotten not by money but by grace, not by bidding with prices but by competition in the display of goodwill."[13] Therefore the intent of the one you have chosen for friendship must be tested acutely, lest your friend desire to be joined with you simply out of hope for some kind of practical gain, thinking friendship more a matter of commerce than of grace.

This is why friendships among the poor are far more certain than those of the rich, since poverty removes the hope of gain from a friendship, so that it does not diminish but rather increases the love of the friendship.

71. And so people oblige the rich so as to flatter them, but no one is disingenuous to a poor person. Whatever

---

13 Ambrose, *On the Duties of the Clergy*, 3.134.

is granted to a poor person is genuine, because a friendship with a poor person lacks the inducements to envy.[xx] (By this I mean not that we should check a potential friend's social status, but that we should test his character.)

Thus, one tests a friend's intent. If you see that your friend is more desirous of your goods than of yourself, and if he is always after some benefit which your diligence can provide—honor, wealth, glory, or freedom—if for all this you prefer the friendship of someone worthier than he, or (to be sure) if you are not able to provide him with what he seeks, you will easily see his intent in attaching himself to you.

The Test of a Friend's Good Judgement and Patience (3.72–73)

72. And now we should examine judgment. Some people, strangely (not to say impudently) enough, "wish to have as a friend the sort of person they themselves are incapable of being."[14] Such people are those who are impatient with their friends' minor transgressions, who rebuke them sternly and, because they lack good judgment, neglect important matters while arousing themselves against trivialities. They confuse everything because they have no notion of the proper place, or the right time, or the persons who should or should not be privy to such matters. For this reason, you should test the judgment of the one you choose as a friend; otherwise, if you form a bond of friendship with one who is shortsighted and imprudent, you may find that you have to deal with daily disputes and quarrels.

---

14 Cicero, *On Friendship*, 22.82.

73. Surely this is a virtue of friendship that is easy enough to test, because if anyone lacks good judgement, he is like a ship without a rudder that is constantly carried about by the shifting gusts of wind and the unpredictable motion of the waves (*Eph 4:14*).

In the same way, also, there will be many opportunities to test the patience of one whom you desire to be a friend when it is necessary to correct the one you love. Sometimes it will be good to do this rather more harshly, as though from diligence, so that you may test or exercise his powers of toleration.[xxi]

Concluding Thoughts on Testing a Friendship (3.74–75)

74. This should certainly be attended to, so that if you test your friend and find in him such things as offend your soul, or some careless revelation of a confidence, or a desire for some temporal gain, or a somewhat ill-judged chastisement, or some transgression of the gentleness appropriate to friends, you should not immediately shrink back from your proposed friendship or choice while there is any hope of his correction. You should never tire of being careful in the choice and testing of friends, since the fruit of this labor is "live-saving medicine and mortality's" firmest foundation (Sir 6:16).[15]

75. For since many are skilled in multiplying earthly treasures, in raising, selecting and comparing cattle and asses, sheep and goats, and since there are accurate standards for judging all these animals, it is sheer madness not to take the same care in getting and testing friends, and to learn to recognize the signs which show that those

---

15 Aelred paraphrases Sir 6:16 here.

we have chosen for friendship are indeed worthy of it. We must certainly be careful of that impulse of love that "rushes ahead of judgement" and removes the ability to test one's friends.[16]

---

16 Cicero, *On Friendship*, 18.65.

Discussion Questions

 Aelred believed in the principle that "all truth is God's truth." He was not afraid to use truth found in pagan writers like Cicero. One example is that when a friendship needs to be ended, it "should be unstitched little by little" so as to preserve as much of the friendship as possible (3.41). What principles about friendship can you learn from today's world? What wisdom can be gleaned from literature, psychology, neuroscience, sociology, film, or other places about lasting friendship?

 What do you think about Aelred's practical suggestions about how to test a friend's loyalty in 3.65–66? Have you ever tested a friend's loyalty to see if you could rely on him or her?

 Aelred explains that spiritual friendship includes four things: love, affection, security, and delight" (3.51). Love is the foundation of all relationships for a Christian, but spiritual friendship especially includes affection, security, and delight. Aelred explains that "affection" means an "inner pleasure" in your friend, "security" means that you can trust your friend with your heart's secrets, and "delight" means that there is a joyful meeting of minds about all kinds of things. Where have you felt these three emotions in a friendship? Where have you experienced friendships with these kinds of feelings?

Have you ever intentionally tested a friend or potential friend for the four characteristics suggested by Aelred: faithfulness (3.62–67), intentions (3.68–71), good judgement (3.72), or patience (3.73)? If so, how did the test go? Would you pass these tests if someone was testing you for a possible friendship?

In 3.75, Aelred uses an analogy from the business world to argue that we should take at least as much care about investing in friendship as we do when making financial investments. What habits are important for making wise financial decisions? How are these habits similar or different from those needed to form wise friendships?

Chapter 7

Accepting and Enjoying Spiritual Friends (Book 3.76–97)

Chapter Summary

Can you imagine a world where you had no friends? Could you be happy in this kind of world? Chapter 7 continues Aelred's third conversation about spiritual friendship and provides his answers to these two questions (3.76–78). He then shows how God created friendship to fill all creation with happiness (3.79–81). Aelred describes his own experience of friendship within a loving community of disciples (3.82–84) and answers some practical questions. Walter is a bit overwhelmed by the high aim of spiritual friendship and wonders about settling for a lower version (3.85). Aelred encourages him that lesser forms of friendship are often used by God to lead believers to higher and holier friendships (3.86–87). After giving some more general advice on friendship (3.88–89), Aelred explains how true friendship makes two people equal (3.90–91), and he discusses the friendship between David and Jonathan as evidence (3.92–96).

Text

Without Friendship There Is No Pleasure in Life (3.76–78)

76. AELRED: Just so, it is the task of a prudent man to wait, to rein in this impulse, to affirm the way of good will, to proceed little by little into affection, until finally he may give and dedicate himself totally to his tried and true friend.

WALTER: I must confess that I am still moved by the opinion of those who think that one can live more safely without friends of this sort.

AELRED: This is astounding, since without friends there is absolutely no pleasure in life.

WALTER: But why, I ask you?

77. AELRED: Pretend that the whole human race has been removed from the world, and that you alone have been left as a survivor. And behold, before you are all the delights and riches of the world—gold, silver, precious stones, walled cities, camps and towers, large buildings, statues, paintings. Or think of yourself as transformed to mankind's former state, with all things subject to you, "all sheep and oxen, and also the beasts of the field, the birds of the heavens, and the fish of the sea, whatever passes along the paths of the seas" (Ps 8:7–8; *Gen 1:28*). Now tell me, please, whether you could take pleasure in these things without a companion.

WALTER: Not at all.

78. AELRED: What if there was one other person left, whose language you did not understand, whose ways you did not know, and whose heart and love were concealed from you?

WALTER: If I could not make a friend of this person by sign language of some sort, I would prefer that there be no other person left, rather than one of this sort.

AELRED: But if there were another survivor whom you loved just as you love yourself, and you had no doubt that this person returned your love, wouldn't all the things which before seemed bitter now appear sweet and enjoyable?

WALTER: Yes, indeed.

AELRED: And would it not be the case that, the more such people you had, the happier you would judge yourself to be?

WALTER: That's quite true.

God Designed Friendship to
Fill Creation with Happiness (3.79–81)

79. AELRED: This is that great and wondrous happiness which we look for, when God himself is at work and pouring forth such great friendship and love between himself and his creation—which he has sustained, among the grades and orders which he has distinguished between his creatures, among each of the individual creatures and those he has chosen—that each loves the other as he loves himself. And through this friendship each one rejoices in the happiness of another as much as in his own; and so the happiness of individuals is the happiness of all, and the universality of the happiness of all becomes the happiness of individuals.

80. In the state of happiness there is no concealment of thoughts, no dissimulation of affection. This is what true and eternal friendship is: it takes shape here, in this world, and is perfected in the next; here it is the property of the few who are good; there, where all are good, it is the property of all. Here, where the wise and foolish are mingled together, a time of testing is necessary; there, friends need no testing, since they have been blessed by a certain angelic and (so to speak) divine perfection. Therefore, after this example, let us unite with friends whom we love just as we love ourselves, all of whose affairs are revealed to us, to whom we in turn reveal all of our own secrets; those who are steadfast and stable and constant in all things should be our friends.

Do you think that any mortal does not wish to be loved?

WALTER: I don't think so.

81. AELRED: If you saw someone who lived with many other people, but was suspicious of them all, as though he feared they were plotting against his life, and thought no one loved him, would you not consider this man most wretched?

WALTER: I would consider him most wretched indeed.

AELRED: So also you will not deny that the man who is dear to the hearts of those with whom he lives, who loves all and is loved by all, who enjoys the sweetest tranquility and therefore is not riven by suspicion or struck by fear—surely you will agree that this is the happiest man?

WALTER: You have spoken most excellently and truly.

A Practical Example of the Joy of Friendship within a Loving Community of Disciples (3.82–84)

82. AELRED: But if somehow it is difficult to find such a one among all of those who are now alive (since this sort of perfection is reserved for our future), will we consider ourselves happier to the extent that people with such qualities as these are more numerous among us? When I was walking around the monastery cloister three days ago, as the beloved crowd of brothers was sitting together in a circle, I marveled as though walking among the pleasures of paradise, enjoying the leaves, flowers, and fruits of each single tree. I found not one brother in that whole multitude whom I did not love, and by whom I did not think I was loved in turn; and so I was filled with joy so great that it surpassed all the delights of this world. Indeed, I felt as though my spirit had been poured into all of them, and their affection had been transplanted into me, so that I could say with the prophet, "Behold, how good and pleasant it is, when brothers dwell in unity" (Ps 133:1).

GRATIAN: Are we to believe that you have received into friendship all those whom you love thus, and who love you in return?

83. AELRED: We embrace many with every sort of affection whom we still do not admit to the inner secrets of our friendship, which after all consists mostly in the revelation of all our inmost secrets and counsels. And so the Lord says in the Gospel, "No longer do I call you servants . . . but I have called you friends" and adding the reason why the disciples were considered worthy of the name of friend he said, "for all that I have heard from my

Father I have made known to you" (John 15:15). Also, "You are my friends if you do what I command you" (John 15:14). Concerning these words the blessed Ambrose said,

> He gave the form of friendship which we should follow, that we do the will of our friend, that we reveal our secrets to our friend, whatever we have in our heart, and that we should not be unaware of our friend's own secrets. Let us reveal ourselves to him, and let him open his heart to us. For a friend hides nothing. If he is a true friend, he pours forth his soul, just as the Lord Jesus poured forth the mysteries of his Father.[1]

84. This is what Ambrose said. Therefore, how many people do we love to whom it would be unwise to lay open our soul and to pour forth our inmost being—I mean those whose age or sensibility or judgment is not strong enough to bear the weight of such revelations.

Simple Earthly Friendships Can Grow into Spiritual Friendships (3.85–87)

85. WALTER: This friendship is so sublime and perfect that I do not dare to aspire to it. The friendship that Augustine described is enough for Gratian here and me—that is, to speak and laugh together, and to yield to each other in mutual goodwill; to read and to compare notes together, to be lighthearted or serious together;[xxii] sometimes to disagree (but without hatred as a man might disagree with himself) and by that very infrequent disagreement to enliven our far more frequent agreements; to teach or learn something from each other; to long for absent

---

1   Ambrose, *On the Duties of the Clergy*, 3.136.

friends with uneasy hearts, and to welcome returning friends with joy.

86. By these and by other signs of this sort, proceeding from the hearts of those who love and love in return, by facial expressions, by words, by glances of the eyes and a thousand other pleasing gestures, as though to fuse the souls of friends together over a fire, and to make of many one: this is what we think should be loved in friends, to the end that it appears our consciences stand condemned if we fail to give and receive love mutually (*1 John 4:11*).

87. AELRED: This is fleshly friendship, the sort that is most common among the young, which is what Augustine and his friend were at the time of which he was speaking.[2] Still, with the exception of its trifles and its falsehoods, and if there is in it nothing dishonorable, we must tolerate this type of friendship in the hope of some more abundant grace, as if it were the beginnings of a holier type of friendship. By these beginnings, and with the growth of religious feeling and equality of the spiritual zeal shown by friends, also with the seriousness that increases with age, and with the illumination of their spiritual sensibilities, with a purer affection they may ascend to higher things, as though leaving behind their old familiar haunts. It is as we said yesterday, that one can make a rather easy transition from human friendship to friendship with God himself, because of the similarity between the two.

---

2   Fleshly friendships were discussed during the first conversation; see Chapter 2 (1.38–41).

Friendship Is the Spice of Life, but Beware of Poisons (3.88–89)

88. But now it is time for us to examine how friendship is to be cultivated. "Faithfulness, then, is the foundation of stability and constancy in friendship: for there is nothing stable which is faithless."[3] Therefore in their mutual relationships, friends ought to be simple, courteous, and agreeable;[xxiii] moreover, they ought to be such as to be moved by these qualities in others. Now, all these qualities have to do with faithfulness, for the temperament that is characterized by faith cannot be devious and crafty. Nor can those who are unmoved by the same qualities or who disagree about these qualities be stable or faithful to each other.

89. However, we must avoid suspicion before all else—it is poison to a friendship—so that we never harbor evil thoughts about a friend, nor give credence to or go along with someone who makes slanderous remarks about our friend.

At this point in our conversation I should deal with agreeableness, cheerfulness in expression, attractiveness of personality, the peacefulness one finds even in a glance—all of these are no little part of what makes friendship the spice of life. For a sober and rather grave facial expression has a certain honorable dignity, to be sure, but sometimes "friendship ought to be a little loose," as it were, and "freer and more pleasant, more prone to fellowship and ease" though without flightiness and license.[4]

---

3   Cicero, On Friendship, 18.65.

4   Ibid., 18.66.

Spiritual Friendship Makes Two People into Equals (3.90–91)

90. Besides, it is a strong point of friendship that the superior becomes equal to the inferior. For often those who are lower in rank, class, dignity, or knowledge are received into friendship by those who outstrip them in some way. In these cases, it is proper for them to despise and to count as nothing, as mere vanity, whatever qualities come from sources other than nature. Instead, they should be mindful of the beauty of friendship, which is not decked out with silks and gems, nor enlarged by possessions or fattened with expensive delicacies, not praised with high honors or inflated with dignities.

And so, returning to the principle of the origin of friendship, they should scrutinize the equality given by nature rather than the baubles which greed afford to mortals.

91. So also in friendship, which is the best gift of both nature and grace, the exalted come down and the lowly climb in status; the wealthy become poor and the poor abound in wealth (1 Sam 2:7–8; Luke 2:52–53); and so each partner shares his state with his friend, with the result that there is equality between them, as Scripture says: "Whoever gathered much had nothing left over, and whoever gathered little had no lack" (Exod 16:18; 2 Cor 8:15). Therefore you should never give yourself preference over your friend; and if by chance you should happen to be your friend's superior in any of those areas I just mentioned, then you should not hesitate to submit yourself to your friend all the more, to show your trust in him and to praise him if he is bashful, and to confer all the more honor upon him to the degree that his condition or poverty dictates that he should be without honor.

David and Jonathan's Friendship Brought Equality between Two Different Social Statuses (3.92–96)

92. For example, Jonathan, the most outstanding of youths, ignored his royal lineage and his expectation of the throne and made a covenant of friendship with David (*1 Sam 20; 23:17*). In friendship he accounted this little servant the equal of his master, and so when David was fleeing from Saul, when he was hiding in the wilderness, condemned to die, Jonathan esteemed before himself this man who was destined for death. Humiliating himself and exalting his friend, he said, "You shall be king over Israel, and I shall be next to you" (1 Sam 23:17). What an outstanding example of true friendship! What a wonderful thing! King Saul was raging against a mere servant, and stirring up the whole country against him as though against a rival for his throne (*1 Sam 23:19–26*); he killed the priests only because he suspected they had betrayed him (*1 Sam 22:18–19*); he marched through the meadows and searched out the vales; he surrounded the high places and cliffs with an armed band; all his men pledged themselves as avengers of the king's anger (*1 Sam 22:6–10; 23:7–8*). Only Jonathan, who alone could have been justly envious, thought that he should oppose his father, defer to his friend, and offer him counsel. And preferring friendship to kingship he said, "You shall be king over Israel, and I shall be next to you" (1 Sam 23:17).

93. And see how Jonathan's father stirred up his son's envy against his friend by pressing him with insults, terrifying him with threats, reminding him that he would be denied his kingdom and deprived of his honor. For when he had pronounced sentence of death upon David, Jonathan did not fail his friend: "Why should he be put

to death?" he asked. "What was his sin? What has he done? For he took his life in his hand and he struck down the Philistine . . . you saw it and rejoiced. Why then shall he die?" (1 Sam 19:4–5; 20:32).[5] On hearing this the king became insane with anger and tried to pin Jonathan to the wall with his lance, adding this insult to his threat: "You son of a perverse, rebellious woman, do I not know that you have chosen the son of Jesse to your own shame, and to the shame of your mother's nakedness?" (1 Sam 20:30).

Jonathan Takes Aim to Warn His Friend David

94. Then he poured forth all the venom he could to bespatter the young man's heart, adding this as an incitement to ambition, as kindling for envy and incentive for zeal and bitterness: "For as long as the

---

5   Aelred paraphrases and combines 1 Sam 19:4–5 and 20:32 here.

son of Jesse lives on the earth, neither you nor your kingdom shall be established" (1 Sam 20:31). Who would not be moved by these words, who would not become envious? Whose love, favor, and friendship would they not corrupt, threaten, and destroy? But this young man most lovingly preserved the laws of friendship and showed himself proof against threats, patient against insults, and all for friendship's sake disdainful of the king, heedless of glory, but mindful of grace. "You shall be king over Israel," he said, "and I shall be next to you" (1 Sam 23:17).

95. "Some have been found," says Cicero, who "think it shameful to prefer money to friendship," but it is impossible to find those "who do not rank offices, magistracies, empires, power, and wealth higher than friendship. The result is that, once these worldly things have been set before them on one side and the power of friendship has been set on the other, they prefer the worldly things by far. For human nature is feeble when it comes to spurning power; where," Cicero asks, "will you find someone who would place the honor of his friend before his own?"[6]

96. This is that true, perfect, stable, and eternal friendship which envy cannot corrupt, suspicion cannot diminish, and ambition cannot dissolve. Even though it is tested, it does not cease; even if it is battered as by Saul, it does not fall into pieces; when it is struck by so many insults, it shines through as steadfast, and it remains immovable no matter how many injuries it has suffered. Therefore, "go and do likewise" (Luke 10:37).

However, if you think it difficult or even impossible to give preference to the one you love over yourself, you

---

6 Cicero, *On Friendship*, 17.63–64.

should not neglect to make your friend your equal, if you really wish to be a friend.

97. For those who do not maintain equality do not rightly cultivate friendship. Ambrose said, "Defer to a friend as you would to an equal; do not be ashamed to outstrip your friend in doing good. For friendship knows no pride."[7] And so "faithful friends are life-saving medicine, and the grace of immortality" (Sir 6:16).[8]

[3.97 continues in the next chapter.]

---

7 Ambrose, *On the Duties of the Clergy,* 3.129.

8 Aelred paraphrases Sir 6:16 here.

Discussion Questions

What do you think about Aelred's thought experiment in 3.76–78? Can you imagine a world with no friendship? Do you agree that friendships are as important to living the kind of life God created humans to live as Aelred seems to think?

What do you think about Aelred's eschatological[9] approach to Christian friendship (3.79–80)? He suggests that eventually we will be friends with everyone in heaven, but for now our finitude and human sinfulness means that we must be satisfied with a smaller group of friends. Does his logic make sense to you?

Aelred is articulate about the feelings of love he experienced as he walked around looking at different members of his discipleship community (3.82–84). When have you experienced feelings like Aelred describes? Does Aelred's distinction between those he loves and those who are his trusted friends within the community make sense to you? Do you see any potential problems with it?

Aelred calls friendship the spice of life, and reminds us that sometimes friends need to "be a little loose" (3.89). What are ways that you relax and loosen up with friends? How often do you take time to just have fun with your friends and enjoy God's good gift of friendship?

---

9 Eschatology – the study of the "eschaton," or the end times.

One of the reasons God gave the Sabbath was so his people could enjoy the gift of friendship. How could you use the Sabbath to enjoy friends? There are many places in Scripture where we are called to "guard" the sabbath. Is there a time on your sabbath day, or another time during your week, which you can "guard" for spending time with friends?

CHRISTIAN MINISTRY

Chapter 8

Giving and Receiving between Spiritual Friends (Book 3.97–134)

Chapter Summary

There is a right time to correct a friend, and a time to be silent (Job 2:11–13). This chapter's practical instructions include wisdom on how to know the difference between the two. It concludes Aelred's final conversation about spiritual friendship. In the last chapter, Aelred discussed the joy and happiness that spiritual friendship brings to those who experience it. In this chapter, he talks about several practical topics related to friendship. First, spiritual friends are generous to one another with both tangible and intangible assets (3.97–103); Aelred reminds us that a "friend in need is a friend indeed." He then talks about the importance of speaking the truth in love to a friend when a friend is in the wrong (3.104–109). Aelred believes that giving loving correction is one of the most important gifts friends can give one another, but he also shows that the timing and location of the correction are important (3.109–113).

Aelred then deals with a practical challenge to which those in positions of power and influence within the church will relate. He addresses the question of how and when one should give promotions and positions of leadership to your friends (3.114–118). Aelred shows how these principles work practically by telling a story about two of his friends and how he related to them when opportunities to serve in leadership arose (3.119–127). The chapter ends with a final summary, and a reminder that the goal of all spiritual friendship is to help spiritual friends grow in their friendship with God, a friendship that will one day be made complete in heaven (3.128–134).

Text

Friends Are Generous with One Another (3.97–100)

97. (cont.) AELRED: And now let us examine how friendship is to be cultivated in the doing of favors. Here let us steal an insight from another's hands. Someone said, "Let this law be sanctified in friendship, that from friends we seek what is honorable, that for friends we do what is honorable, and that we not wait to be asked to do this service. Let there never be any delay, let us always be zealous in this."[1]

98. If we are expected to expend our money on behalf of our friends, how much more should we take account of our friends' advantages and needs! But everyone cannot do everything: one man has money in abundance, another has lands and possessions, a third has the gift

---

1   Cicero, *On Friendship*, 13.44.

of counsel, and yet another excels more in his positions of honor. In all these instances you should carefully consider what sort of person you should reveal yourself to be to your friend. Scripture deals well enough with money: "Lose your silver for the sake of a brother or a friend," it says (Sir 29:10). But since a wise man has eyes in his head (*Eccl 2:14*), we should do what the prophet says if we are ourselves members of the body and Christ is the head (*Eph 1:22–23; 5:30; Col 1:18*): "My eyes are ever toward the Lord" (Ps 25:15); we should do this so that we can receive from him that formula for living about which it is written, "If any of you lacks wisdom, let him ask God, who gives generously to all without reproach" (Jas 1:5).

99. So you should give to a friend so as not to reproach him; do not look for gain in return; do not wrinkle your forehead, nor look the other way nor avert your eyes. Rather, with a serene and happy expression, and with pleasant speech, you should anticipate the request of a friend in need; help him with all goodwill, so that it seems you are granting his request without being asked. A man of honest spirit thinks nothing more embarrassing than to ask for a favor. Therefore, although there should be "one heart and soul" (Acts 4:32) between you and your friend, it is very harmful to your friendship if there is not also "one purse."

Therefore, this law should hold among friends in this matter, that they expend both themselves and their material goods in such a way that the one who gives maintains his cheerfulness, while the one who receives does not thereby lose his security.

100. When Boaz noticed the poverty of Ruth the Moabite, he spoke to her as she was gleaning behind his harvesters; he consoled her, he invited her to eat with his servants, and he honestly spared her feelings by ordering his harvesters intentionally to leave behind some ears of grain, which she could glean without shame (*Ruth 2:8–9*). So we also should discretely discover the needs of our friends and anticipate their requests by doing them favors, meanwhile giving in such a way that he who receives the favor appears to be doing the good deed, rather than he who does the favor.[2]

How Does Friendship Work When You Have Nothing Material to Give? (3.100–103)

WALTER: But we are permitted neither to receive nor to give away possession; how will this grace of spiritual friendship hold among us?[3]

101. AELRED: The wise man says that "men would lead the happiest life if they would get rid of these two words, 'my' and 'your.'"[4] It is certain that a sanctified poverty offers much soundness to spiritual friendship, for although greed is destructive to friendship, once friendship is born it is certainly more easily preserved to the extent that the heart is found to be more pure of that contagion. However, there are other benefits in spiritual love, with which friends

---

2   Aelred implies that Boaz and Ruth were friends. This was a revolutionary idea in the ancient world where many did not believe it was possible for men and women to be friends.

3   Walter, Gratian, and Aelred were members of a Benedictine community of Christian disciples who had taken a vow of poverty that prevented them from owning personal property. See Peters, *Becoming a Community of Disciples* for more information about this commitment.

4   Pseudo-Seneca, *Monita*, 97.

can render aid to each other. The first benefit is that friends are concerned for each other, pray for each other, one blushes for the other, another rejoices for the other, one mourns the fall of the other as he would his own, another regards the advantage of the other as his own (*Rom 12:15*).

102. A friend uses whatever means he can to encourage the timid, strengthen the weak, console the sad, and check the enraged (*Rom 12:15; 1 Cor 9:22; 1 Thess 5:14*). Besides, one ought to have such regard for the eyes of his friends, that he dares to do nothing which is not honorable, to say nothing which is unbecoming.[xxiv] For the matters in which he fails taint his friends also, so that not only the sinner himself blushes and grieves within himself, but also the friend who sees or hears the sin blames himself as though he himself had sinned. Therefore, the friend thinks that not he himself, but the sinner, should be spared. And so respect[xxv] is the best companion of friendship, and for that reason "he who deprives friendship of respect takes away its greatest ornament."[5]

103. How often a mere nod from my friend either stifled or stopped completely the anger which had flamed up in my heart and begun to break forth into public view! How many times did his stern gaze prevent me from uttering the unbecoming word that was already on the tip of my tongue! How often, when I had quite carelessly fallen into raucous laughter or into idleness, did I recover a fitting dignity when my friend entered the room! Moreover, whenever we must be convinced of a course of action, we are quite easily and securely persuaded by friends,

---

5   Cicero, *On Friendship*, 25.91.

in whose arguments there is great authority, since we neither doubt their good faith nor suspect them of flattery.

Spiritual Friends Correct One Another (3.104–109)

104. One friend should therefore attempt to persuade another only of what is honorable, safe, palpable, and free. Nor should friends only be admonished but they should also be corrected, if there is need. Although the truth is painful to some, if hatred comes from it (as the saying has it, "Indulgence begets friends, but truth begets hatred, although this indulgence is far more harmful, since by being gentle toward sins one allows a friend to fall headlong into great danger")—although, as I say, the truth is painful to some, a friend is most blameworthy and hence especially to be corrected, if he scorns the truth and by his indulgence and gentleness compels the other friend into fault.[6] In all things we should preserve moderation, not because we ought to be sweetly indulgent of our friends' faults, but so that our admonitions be without bitterness and our corrections be without abuse.

105. However, in being indulgent and gentle, we should exercise a certain pleasing and honorable friendliness; but flattery, that nursemaid of vice, ought to be far removed from our gentleness: it is unworthy not only of a friend, but also of a free man. But if one is completely deaf to the truth, such that he simply cannot hear the truth from his friend, then we must despair of his salvation.

106. Therefore, as Ambrose says,

> If you discover any fault in a friend, correct him in private; if he will not listen to you, correct him again. For there is

---

6 Terence, *Andria*, 68.

such a thing as good correction, and it is much better by far than a silent friendship. Even if your friend thinks you are doing him harm, correct him still. For a wounded friend is more bearable than shows of affection from flatterers (*Prov 27:6*). Therefore, correct your erring friend. [7]

However, above all else, you should avoid mental anger and bitterness in correcting a friend, lest you seem to be bent on venting your own spleen rather than truly correcting your friend. [8]

107. For I have seen some people veil long held bitterness and raging anger under the pretense of zeal and freedom in correcting their friends; by following impulse rather than reason they never do good by administering such correction; instead, they are more often an impediment to moral correction.

But among friends there is no excuse for this vice. For one friend ought to be compassionate to another, he ought to condescend, to consider his friend's fault his own. He should correct humbly and compassionately. Indeed, his rather sad expression, his sorrowful voice should administer the correction; his tears should interrupt his words, so that his friend not only sees but also feels in his heart that the correction comes from love and not from rancor. If by chance your friend rejects your first correction, give him a second. Meanwhile, beseech and lament, bearing a sad expression on your face, but maintaining a pious affection for your friend.

---

7 Ambrose, *On the Duties of the Clergy*, 3.128.

8 Venting your spleen – an idiom implying that you are trying to get rid of your own feelings of anger by attacking someone else.

108. You should even search out the quality of your friend's heart, for there are some people who benefit from gentleness, and such friends as these give assent to a gentle correction rather freely. But there are others who will consider nothing of this sort of correction, whom it is easier to correct with a blow or a word. In short, one friend should so conform and adapt himself to another that he fits in well with his friend's disposition (*Rom 12:15; 1 Thess 5:14*); and just as we should aid a friend in times of external adversity, we should hasten to his aid all the more quickly in times of spiritual hardship. Therefore, just as

mutual admonition is proper in friendship, so also it is proper in friendship for one to administer admonition freely, not harshly, and for the other to receive it patiently, not unwillingly. This rule must hold, that there is no greater plague in friendship than flattery and ingratiating behavior.[9]

These are the traits of flighty and deceitful men, those who say everything to please their audience and nothing for the sake of truth.

109. So there should be no hesitation among friends, no deceit, which is the failing most repugnant to friendship. Therefore, we owe a friend "the truth, without which the name of friendship cannot prevail."[10] The holy David said, "Let a righteous man strike me—it is a kindness; let him rebuke me—it is oil for my head" (Ps 141:5). A clever liar provokes the anger of God, and so the Lord says through the prophet, "O my people, your guides mislead you and they have swallowed up the course of your paths" (Isa 3:12). As Solomon said, "With his

---

9 Cicero, *On Friendship*, 25.91.

10 Ibid., 25.92.

mouth the godless man would destroy his neighbor"
(Prov 11:9; *Ps 55:20–21*). Thus, friendship should be
so cultivated that under certain circumstances, perhaps,
dissimulation is permissible, but never simulation.[11]

Wait for the Proper Time to Correct Your Friend (3.109–113)

WALTER: But how can dissimulation be necessary, since
it is always a vice, as I see it?

110. AELRED: You are deceived, my son. For God is said
"to dissimulate the sins" of the delinquent (Wis 11:23),
not desiring "the death of the wicked, but that the wicked
turn from his way and live" (Ezek 33:11).

WALTER: Distinguish, please, between simulation and
dissimulation.

111. AELRED: Simulation, as it seems to me, is a rather
deceptive agreement which is entered into against one's
reasonable judgment. Terence expressed this accurately
enough in the character of Gnatho: "Does someone say
'no'? Then I say 'no.' Does someone say 'yes'? Then I say
'yes.' In short, I have compelled myself to be agreeable in
everything."[12] Perhaps this pagan author has borrowed
these things from our own storehouse of examples, since
he has expressed in words the meaning our prophet
intended to convey. For it is clear that the prophet said
this same thing in the person of the Israelites who had
gone astray: "Do not see . . . speak to us smooth things"
(Isa 30:10). And elsewhere: "The prophets prophesy
falsely, and the priests rule at their direction; my people

---

11 Dissimulation – temporary concealment of one's true thoughts or feelings;
putting on a pretense. Simulation – activity that is intended to deceive.

12 Terence, *Eunuchus*, 252–53.

love to have it so" (Jer 5:31). This vice should be everywhere detested, always and everywhere avoided.

112. Dissimulation, on the other hand, is a certain way of dispensing with, or delaying, either a penalty or a correction, because of place, time, or the person involved— even though it may be against your better judgment. For if a friend should somehow transgress in public, he should not be immediately and openly corrected, but rather you should dissemble, considering the place; and indeed, as far as possible without lying, you should excuse what your friend did, while waiting to administer the correction until the two of you are alone together. So, at a time when the mind is preoccupied with many things, when it is less able to think of what should be said under the circumstances, or when because of external reasons the friend's sensibilities are a little more stirred up because of some trouble, then, under these circumstances, one needs to dissimulate until the friend's inner turmoil is settled and he can give your correction a more peaceful reception.

113. So, when King David was hindered in his lust and added murder to his adultery, the prophet Nathan deferred to the royal majesty when he was about to correct him. So he did not drive home his charge suddenly or with his mind in awe of the king's great person; instead, he prudently relied on a fitting dissimulation and elicited from the king his own condemnation of himself (2 Sam 12:1–15).

Should One Give Promotions to Your Friends (3.114–118)

114. WALTER: I find this distinction very pleasing, but I wish to know this: Suppose a man of some power is able to promote to high offices and other such dignities

whomever he wishes, should he give preference in such promotions to those whom he loves and by whom he is loved? And even among his friends should he promote those whom he loves more ahead of those whom he loves less?

115. AELRED: In this matter also, it is worthwhile to investigate how friendship ought to be cultivated. For there are some who think that they are not loved because it is not possible for them to receive preferment; and they pretend that they are looked down on, if they are not involved with responsibilities and duties. For this reason, we know that no small disputes have arisen among those who count themselves as friends, so that alienation followed indignation, and abuse followed alienation. And so in the matter of dignities and offices, and especially in church offices, you must exercise great caution, and be attentive not to what advancement you can confer, but to what the friend to whom you offer the advancement is able to bear.[xxvi]

116. For there are many who are to be loved, but who need not therefore be given preferment; and we laudably and sweetly embrace many whom we still may not place in positions of responsibility and difficulty without involving ourselves in grave sin and them in the greatest danger. For this reason, in these matters we should follow our heads rather than our hearts; and we should impose such an honor (or burden) not on those whom we consider closer friends, but upon those whom we consider more fit to handle the responsibility. Still, where we find there are equal qualifications, I do not greatly disapprove if one's affection takes account of its own preferences.

117. For this reason no one should say that he is despised because he has not received advancement: although the Lord Jesus preferred Peter to John in this matter, he did not therefore withdraw his affection from John just because he had given Peter the place of authority among the disciples. To Peter he commended the church, to John he entrusted his dearest mother (*John 19:26–27; 21:15–17*). To Peter he gave the keys of his kingdom, for John he saved the secrets of his heart (*Matt 16:19; John 13:23*). Therefore, Peter was given a higher rank, but John was more secure. Peter, then, was endowed with authority when Jesus said, "One of you will betray me," while John, leaning on Jesus' bosom, was made the bolder, when he asked at Peter's signal who would betray him (John 13:21–25). Therefore, Peter is set forth for action, while John is reserved for affection, because Jesus said, "If it is my will that he remain until I come, what is it to you?" (John 21:22). For he has given us an example, that we ourselves should do likewise (*John 13:15*).[13]

118. We should show our friends whatever love, favor, sweetness, and Christian love we can; but let us impose these empty honors and burdens only upon those whom reason dictates, knowing that a man never truly loves his friend if his friend does not suffice without enriching him with these low and contemptible honors besides. However, we should take special caution lest a rather tender affection "impede a greater utility," such as would happen when we wish neither to estrange nor to burden those whom we embrace with greater Christian love, when we see that there is obviously a great hope of richer fruit.[14]

---

13 Aelred paraphrases John 13:15 here.

14 Cicero, *On Friendship*, 20.75.

For this is what well-ordered friendship is, that reason rule the heart, and that we should look not so much to what will make our friends agreeable as to what is most useful for all.

Examples from Two of Aelred's Spiritual Friends (3.119–127)

119. I am thinking now of my two friends who, although taken from this present world, nevertheless to me "live still and will always live."[15] The first of these I joined to myself when I was first converted, because of a certain similarity between our characters and because we followed the same pursuits; the other I chose almost from the time of his boyhood, and after testing him in many different ways I took him into the highest friendship when my advancing age was already turning my hair gray. At a time when I had no burden of pastoral care and was not filled with concern for temporal affairs, I chose the first friend as a partner and companion in the spiritual sweetness and delights of the cloister, into which I was then being initiated. I asked nothing and offered nothing except what Christian love demanded as a sign of that affection. Now in the case of the younger man, once I had taken him on as one of my responsibilities, I had him as a coworker in my labors. Looking back on these friendships, as memory leads me to do, I see that the first depended more on affection and the second on reason, although the first was certainly not lacking in reason, nor was the second bereft of affection.

120. In short, since my first friend was taken from me at the very beginning of our friendship, I was able to choose him as I described, but not to test him.

---

15 Ibid., 27.102.

The other was entrusted to me from his boyhood all the way to middle age, and so I chose him for friendship, and with me he ascended through all the steps of friendship, as far as human frailty in these matters permitted. It was my contemplation of his virtues that first inclined my affection toward him and I brought him from his southern home to this northern solitude and first instructed him in the regular disciplines. From that time he was a victor over the concerns of the body, and able to endure hard work and fasting; and so he was an example for nearly all, a source of admiration for many, and for me he was a glory and a delight. Already then I thought that he should be nourished in the elements of friendship, since I saw that he was a burden to nobody, but instead a delight to all.

121. He would come and go, zealously attentive to the commands of his betters, humble, mild, serious in character, rarely speaking, knowing nothing of indignation and ignorant of grumbling, rancor, and disparagement. He walked "like a deaf man; [he does] not hear, like a mute man who does not open his mouth," he "was like a beast," following the reins in obedience and tirelessly bearing with body and mind the yoke of regular discipline (Pss 38:13; 73:22). Once when he was yet a youth he entered the infirmary, but he was corrected by his holy father (my predecessor) for having so quickly devoted himself, while yet so young, to rest and ease; he blushed so that he soon left the infirmary, and he devoted himself so fervently to physical labor that for many years he gave himself no break from his customary rigor, even when he was urged to do so because of ill health.

122. These things made him very near to my heart in many ways, and so gave me the notion to make him, first,

a partner instead of an inferior, then a friend instead of
a partner, and finally a very close friend indeed. For when
I saw that he had come into the first rank of those
marked by virtue and grace, on the advice of the brothers
I imposed upon him the burden of the subpriorship.[16]
Although he was quite unwilling to accept this post, he
modestly undertook it because he had devoted himself
to total obedience. Still, he asked me many times, when
we were alone, to be relieved of the position, offering as
his excuse his age, his lack of knowledge, and the friendship,
which we had begun, lest by chance this office become
the occasion for our mutual love to diminish.

123. But he got nowhere with these excuses, and so
he began to speak openly and freely (though humbly and
modestly) with me about the things that he feared for
each one of us, and about things in me that he was less
than pleased with. He was hoping, as he later confessed
to me, that I would be offended by his presumption and
so be the more inclined to grant him that which he was
seeking—relief from the burden of authority. But this
freedom with which he spoke his mind only added to the
sum of our friendship, and I wanted him for a friend no
less than before. Then, perceiving that I looked with favor
upon what he said, and that I had answered each of his
points in humility and dealt with them all to his satisfaction,
he saw that he himself had not only garnered no ill will
from his free speech but had even reaped more abundant
fruit; therefore he began to love me more warmly than
he himself used to, to "loosen the reins" of his affection,

---

16 Subprior – the assistant to the monastery prior, a leader in the religious
community.

and to pour himself totally into my heart.[17] So also I made a test of his freedom to speak, and he tested my patience as well.

124. I also, repaying my friend in kind thought that he should be corrected rather severely on one occasion; and although I did not spare the blame, as it were, I found him to be neither impatient of my liberty nor ungrateful. I began then to reveal to him the secrets of my counsels, and he proved himself faithful. So love increased between us, our affection grew warmer, and our Christian love was strengthened until it got to the point that there was in us "one heart and soul, agreement in likes and dislikes" (Acts 4:32),[18] and this love was free of fear (*1 John 4:18*), ignorant of offense, utterly lacking in suspicion, recoiling from flattery (*1 Cor 13:4–7*).

125. Between us there was nothing faked, there was no simulation, no disgraceful fawning, no unbecoming hardness of heart, no beating around the bush, no furtiveness, but we were open and aboveboard in everything. After a fashion, I considered my own heart to be his, and his to be mine, and he himself felt likewise. So as we progressed in our friendship as though in a straight line, neither of us felt indignation when corrected, and neither blamed the other when yielding to his friend. And proving himself a friend in all things, he looked out for my peace and quiet, as far as he could: for my sake he opposed himself to dangers, and he turned aside scandals as they emerged.

126. When he was already growing weak I once wanted to offer him some relief from his temporal duties but he

---

17 Ibid., 8.45.

18 See *Spiritual Friendship*, 1.40.

refused, adding this as a caution: that our mutual love not be measured out according to some worldly comfort, and that it not be ascribed more to my fleshly affection for him than to his need, with the result that my authority would be diminished.

He was therefore like my own right hand, my eye, the "staff of my old age" (Tob 5:23). He was my spirit's resting place, a sweet comfort in times of grief; when I was tired with labors his loving heart received me, and his counsel refreshed me when I was sunk in sadness and lamentation.

127. When I was stirred up he set me at ease, and when I became angry he calmed me. Whatever sadness came I took to him, so that I could bear more easily with my shoulders joined to his the burden I could not bear by myself. What shall I say then? Is it not a certain share of blessedness so to love and be loved, so to help and be helped, and thus to fly higher, from the sweetness of brotherly Christian love to that more sublime splendor of divine love, and now to ascend the ladder of Christian love to the embrace of Christ himself, and then to descend by the same ladder to the love of one's neighbor, where one may sweetly rest? And so if you see something worthy of imitation in this friendship of ours, which I mentioned for the sake of an example, apply it toward your own perfection.

> *"Is it not a certain share of blessedness so to love and be loved, so to help and be helped?"*

Final Summary and Reminder of the Goal of Spiritual Friendship (3.128–134)

128. But now the sun is setting, and so we should end this conversation of ours. Do not doubt, then, that friendship proceeds from love. Indeed, whoever does not love himself,

how can he love another, since he ought to order the love with which he loves his neighbor by its similarity to the love which makes him dear to himself (*Matt 22:39*)? However, he who demands from himself or orders himself to commit any shameful or dishonorable deed does not really love himself.

129. The first task, therefore, is for each partner in a friendship to make himself morally clean, indulging himself in nothing which is indecent, withholding himself from nothing which is beneficial to this end. By truly loving himself thus, and following this rule, he loves his neighbor also. But because this sort of love joins many people together, he should choose from among them those whom he can admit to the secrets of friendship according to familiar custom, upon whom he can bestow his affection freely, laying bare his heart even to the point of revealing his innermost heart and marrow—that is, the thoughts and intentions of his soul.

130. However, a friend should be chosen not according to the desires of affection, but according to the insight of reason, from the similarity of the friend's character and from a contemplation of his virtues. Then let him so devote himself to his friend that all flightiness is absent, and all joy is present; nor should the expected duties or favors of good will and Christian love be missing, either. And after this, let a friend's good faith be tested, as well as his honesty and patience. Little by little there should come about a sharing of counsels, an application to common pursuits, and a certain conformity of expression.

131. For thus friends should conform to themselves, that immediately when they see each other, even the likeness

of the one's face is transferred to the other, whether the
one is downcast in sadness or serene with joy. Once a friend
has been chosen and tested, you should make certain
that he desires neither to ask from his friend nor, if asked,
to do anything that is unseemly; then, when you have
also assured yourself that he thinks friendship to be a virtue
rather than a material benefit, that he avoids flattery
and hates fawning obedience,[xxvii] that he is free with his
discretion, patient in correction, and steadfast and stable
in love—then, I say, you will experience that spiritual
sweetness, that is, "how good and pleasant it is when
brothers dwell in unity" (Ps 133:1).

132. How useful, then, to grieve for each other, to work
for each other, to bear one another's burdens, when each
friend considers it pleasant to neglect himself for the
other's good—to prefer the other's will to his own, to meet
the other's needs before meeting his own, to oppose his
friend's adversity by interposing himself (*Gal 6:2*)! In the
meantime, how sweet friends consider it to deliberate
together, to open their pursuits to each other, to examine
all things at once, and to come to one opinion about
all things!

133. And then there comes prayer for each other, which,
as one friend remembers another in prayer, is the more
effective as it is directed to God with greater affection,
with the flowing tears either excited by fear, or elicited by
affection, or compelled by grief (*Job 42:8–10*). And so,
praying to Christ on behalf of his friend, and wishing to
be heard by Christ for his friend, he exerts himself
diligently and desirously to be heard; and then, suddenly
and imperceptibly, the affection at some time passes over
to the one loved and, as though touching the sweetness that

is with Christ himself, he begins "to taste how sweet he is" and "to feel how good he is" (Pss 34:8; 100:5).[19]

134. So, ascending from that holy love with which he embraces his friend to that love with which he embraces Christ, he will reap the fruit of spiritual friendship with a face filled with joy, and he will look forward to the fullness of all things in the time to come. When that fear is removed which we now feel and by which we are filled with care for each other, and when all adversity, which we now must bear for each other, is driven away, and especially when the sting of death is destroyed along with death itself (*1 Cor 15:54–55*), by the pangs of which we now must be worn out, so that we must grieve for each other—when all these are past, and security has arrived, we will rejoice in the eternity of that Highest Good, when this friendship to which we here admit only a few is poured out over all, and is poured out by all in turn upon God, and when God is "all in all" (1 Cor 15:28).

---

19 Aelred paraphrases Pss 34:8 and 100:5 here.

Discussion Questions

 Aelred is a realist in that he believes the fallenness and finitude of our present state prevents us from being spiritual friends with all people. But the final sentence in *Spiritual Friendship* (3.134) points to a different situation in the future. Aelred is looking forward to the time "when this friendship to which we here admit only a few is poured out over all, and is poured out by all in turn upon God, and when God is "all in all" (1 Cor 15:28)." Have you thought much about the kind of friendships we will enjoy in heaven? If not, what do you think those friendships will be like? What do you think Aelred would say about the joy of the friendships we will experience in heaven?

 Aelred says that it is very harmful to a friendship if there is not "one purse" between the two (3.99). Do you agree with him on this point? Do you think it was easier for him to live "with one purse" than it is for you and your friends? Do you agree that Aelred's claim is true for friends in a marriage covenant? In what other friendships might Aelred's claim hold true? Where would it not work?

 How would you feel if you had the opportunity to give a promotion to a friend, but he or she was not as well qualified as a different candidate? What emotions would you feel? Would you find Aelred's advice on how to deal with this situation helpful (3.114–118)?

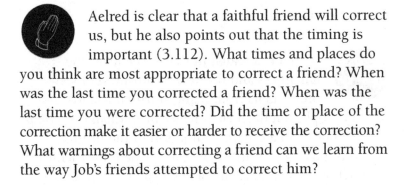

Aelred is clear that a faithful friend will correct us, but he also points out that the timing is important (3.112). What times and places do you think are most appropriate to correct a friend? When was the last time you corrected a friend? When was the last time you were corrected? Did the time or place of the correction make it easier or harder to receive the correction? What warnings about correcting a friend can we learn from the way Job's friends attempted to correct him?

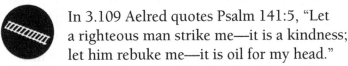

In 3.109 Aelred quotes Psalm 141:5, "Let a righteous man strike me—it is a kindness; let him rebuke me—it is oil for my head." Aelred wants to make sure Christian leaders understand that being corrected by a friend is an important part of spiritual friendship. Where do you regularly open yourself to correction from a friend? How could you develop a habit of opening yourself to receiving faithful wounds from a friend (Prov 27:6)?

Afterword

CHRISTIAN MINISTRY

Afterword

Congratulations on making it all the way through Aelred's *Spiritual Friendship*. It is no small accomplishment to read a book that is over eight hundred years old. It is even a greater accomplishment to read it with a group of friends. I hope you and your friends have had many good conversations while discussing Aelred's insights and recommendations about spiritual friendship.

By way of conclusion, we can glean three big-picture takeaways from Aelred's spiritual classic.

(1) Spiritual friendship is an essential spiritual discipline if one wants to grow into spiritual maturity.

(2) Stewardship of one's soul requires prioritizing spiritual friendship.

(3) We need to implement the practical steps Aelred recommends if we hope to become the kind of person others want to be spiritual friends with and if we hope to develop eternal spiritual friendships with others.

In these three takeaways we can recognize the pattern of Vision, Intention, Means that Dallas Willard describes as basic to all spiritual formation.[1] Below, we briefly explore each.

Vision: I Must Pursue Spiritual Friendship as a Spiritual Discipline

First, Aelred teaches us that friendship is an important spiritual discipline. Repeatedly, Aelred reminds us that spiritual friendships with sisters and brothers are a reliable pathway to friendship with God. Finding a "soul" sister or brother—one who is committed to loving God with their whole self, and who also encourages us to love God with our whole heart—is one of the greatest gifts we can receive on earth. Perhaps reading *Spiritual Friendship* has also opened your eyes to how God can use friendships as a powerful tool to form your soul into maturity? Today we can believe and ask God for the kinds of friendships we read about in Scripture, friendships like those between David and Jonathan, between Ruth and Naomi, or between Jesus and his disciples. We can also look forward to increasing levels of joy and happiness in our life as we gain experience in spiritual friendship (3.76–81).

Intention: I Must Choose to Guard Time and Energy for Spiritual Friendship

Second, Aelred invites us to choose to prioritize spiritual friendship in our schedules and ministry priorities. Think for a minute about the story of the wealthy farmer in Luke 12:15–21. This worker was very smart about managing

---

1   Dallas Willard, *Renovation of the Heart: Putting on the Character of Christ* (Colorado Springs, CO: NavPress, 2002), 82–91.

his work and finances. He was a good steward of time
and energy in many practical ways, and he had a lot of
"good fruit" to show for it. But Jesus warned his hearers
that the worker had neglected one important priority—
his own soul (Luke 12:20). Aelred wants us to understand
that if we desire to build a wise life, spiritual friendship
must be a central part of our foundation (*Matt 7:24–27*).
Do you want to become spiritually mature? If so, are you
willing to change your priorities so that spiritual friendships
can become a significant part of your spiritual formation?

Means: I Must Practice the Steps Aelred Recommends If I Want to Make Spiritual Friendships

Finally, Aelred taught me that there is a great deal of skill
and strategy in making spiritual friends. Like anything
worth doing, we must be willing to practice if we are
going to develop the kind of friendship Aelred describes
in *Spiritual Friendship*. Aelred's four steps of choosing,
testing, accepting, and enjoying spiritual friends are
valuable if we truly desire to make spiritual friends (see his
discussions of these steps in Book 3). His advice and
stories about correcting a friend, and being patient when
your friend corrects you, are essential lessons spiritual
friends must learn (3.104–113). His encouragement to be
generous with your friends is challenging to read today,
especially for those of us who live in the materialistic
culture that pervades North America (3.97–103).

May the Lord bless you as you make spiritual friends on
your journey to the heavenly city, the place where all will
be friends with one another and with God (3.134).

CHRISTIAN MINISTRY

Resources for Application

CHRISTIAN MINISTRY

Soul Work and Soul Care:
Learning to Make Spiritual Friendship a Fine Art
By Hank Voss

No one presumes to teach an art until he has first carefully studied it. Look how foolish it is for the inexperienced to assume pastoral authority, since the care of souls is the art of arts!

~ Gregory the Great, c. 590

Your leaders . . . keep watch over your souls and will give an account for their work.

~ Hebrews 13:17a

Each Sacred Roots Spiritual Classic has a "Soul Work and Soul Care" resource to illustrate how Christian leaders across cultures and generations have found a particular spiritual classic helpful in pastoral ministry. "Soul work" includes the *personal* work of watering, weeding, pruning, and fertilizing the garden of one's own soul. In a similar way, "soul care" involves the *pastoral* work of nurturing growth in another's friendship with God. When Jesus discusses "soul work" and "soul care," he often uses metaphors from the medical and agricultural professions. Like a doctor for souls, or a farmer caring for an orchard of fruit trees, congregational leaders who hope to tend souls can learn much from the wisdom of those who have gone before us.

The *Oikos* Principle and Biblical Examples of Spiritual Friendship

Spiritual friendships are difficult to build and maintain in western culture for at least four reasons. (1) Western culture approaches the world in far more individualistic ways than other cultures and generations.[1] (2) We tend to be very task-oriented and leave little time for nurturing relationships.[2] (3) We tend to sexualize relationships and so limit the possibilities for friendship that were once common.[3] (4) We are far more transitory than previous generations. Making friends takes time, and we often begin to establish friendships only to move and leave them behind. Doubtless we could add additional reasons, but these four challenges to spiritual friendship provide some initial clarity as to why a recovery of Aelred's wisdom about spiritual friendship is vitally important for Christian leaders today.

As we explore spiritual friendship below, please remember that all friendships are a gift from God, especially spiritual friendships. Whether you have many spiritual friendships, or very few, this appendix provides encouragement to make the pursuit of spiritual friendship a high priority in your life and ministry. It begins by looking at findings from social scientist Robin Dunbar and at the example of King David to emphasize the importance of strategically prioritizing

---

1 Simon Chan, *Spiritual Theology: A Systematic Study of the Christian Life* (Downers Grove, IL: IVP Academic, 1998), 174.

2 Klaus Issler, *Wasting Time With God: A Christian Spirituality of Friendship With God* (Downers Grove: IVP, 2001), 255n3; Ajith Fernando, *Reclaiming Friendship: Relating to Each Other in a Frenzied World* (Scottdale, PA: Herald, 1993), 16–17.

3 I disagree with many of Alan Bray's ethical conclusions. But he is surely correct when he writes, "The inability to conceive of relationships in other than sexual terms says something of contemporary poverty ..." (Alan Bray, *The Friend* [Chicago: University of Chicago Press, 2003], 6).

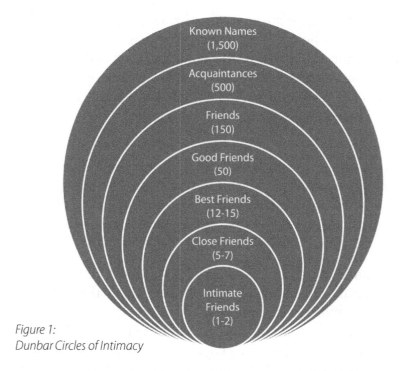

Figure 1:
Dunbar Circles of Intimacy

specific spiritual friendships. It then looks at the life of Jesus and the prioritized pyramid of relationships we see modeled during his earthly ministry and suggests ways Jesus' example can be adapted for Christians today. Finally, it briefly describes five tools for building spiritual friendships from the many that have been used over the past twenty centuries.

Aelred invites us to enjoy the feast of spiritual friendship with some, while welcoming all with Christian love. If he lived today he would be interested in the findings of social scientists like Robin Dunbar. Dunbar has shown that human social networks tend to operate in expanding circles of intimacy (see Figure 1).[4] Aelred would likely agree with

---

4   Robin Dunbar, *Friends: Understanding the Power of Our Most Important Relationships* (New York: Little, Brown, 2022), 56.

these findings about concentric circles and explain that all
earthly relationships are limited by human fallenness or sin
and human finitude, or the amount of time and energy
humans can invest in friendships. Due to these limitations,
Aelred encouraged serious disciples to carefully choose,
test, accept and enjoy their friends (3.8).[5]

Aelred's insistence on careful consideration of who we make
a "guardian of our soul" is wise, and it opens the door to an
important principle of spiritual friendship—we need to
prioritize our relational networks by developing intentional
and thoughtful habits. One way to develop these habits is
through stewarding *oikos* spheres of relationships.

In an important book on kingdom citizenship, Don
Davis describes "the *oikos* factor" as one of "the [six]
most fundamental concepts . . . necessary to Christian
discipleship and ministry."[6] Do not be surprised if the
word *oikos* is new; it is a Greek word important in New
Testament vocabulary and often translated "house" or
"household." It also provides the root for English words
like "economics" and "economy." Davis defines the idea
of *oikos* as an "entire network of relationships that we have
in our immediate and extended families, our friendships,
those connected to our web of contacts and associations."[7]
For Davis, carefully stewarding and intentionally engaging
the *oikos* factor is a central principle of kingdom citizenship.
God calls all disciples to be wise stewards of our various
social circles and spheres of relationships.

---

5   References to *Spiritual Friendship* are noted parenthetically by book and
paragraph number.

6   Don Davis, *Get Your Pretense On! Living as an Ambassador of the Kingdom of
God* (Wichita, KS: The Urban Ministry Institute, 2018), 16.

7   Ibid., 138.

We see examples of intentionally prioritizing friendship in the lives and ministry of biblical leaders. King David, for example, was highly skilled at developing friendships, although he also failed in spectacular fashion—for example when he betrayed one of his friends (Uriah the Hittite), murdered him, and stole his wife, Bathsheba. Yet despite his failures, Scripture describes many of David's friendships: (1) his best friend Jonathan (1 Sam 18); (2) his three close friends, Abishai, Eleazar, and Jashobeam (2 Chron 11:11–21; 2 Sam 23:8–17); (3) his thirty mighty men (1 Chron 12:2–7, 16–18; 1 Sam 23:18–38); (4) his eleven Gadite friends (1 Chron 12:8–15), "his friends the elders" (1 Sam 30:26), the names of a wide variety of influential friends like Hushai (2 Sam 15:37) and Hiram, King of Tyre (1 Kings 5:1), and the personal names of well over one hundred leaders loyal to David and involved in his kingdom (1 Chron 23–27; 2 Chron 12:19–28).

David's valuing and experiences with friendship are not just recorded in stories, but also in psalms and proverbs. David's name is connected to many biblical psalms that talk about friends (e.g. Ps 55). His son, King Solomon, likely observed many lessons about friendship from his dad's example, and is connected with many proverbs about friendship (e.g. Prov 27:6), poetic reflections on friendship (Eccl 4:9–12), and a love story about two friends (Song of Songs). In addition to scriptural texts connected to King David, we could also learn much from Job, Ruth, the Apostle Paul, and many other biblical friendships. Yet perhaps the best scriptural example of investing in friendships and prioritizing relationships come from the life of Jesus of Nazareth.

Like King David, Jesus modeled a diverse group of friendships, although Jesus broadened his friendship circles beyond King David's in order to include many women. Even today, Jesus is willing to call "friend" any disciple who obeys his commandments (John 15:14). Figure 2 reveals that Jesus, while on earth and limited by human finitude, chose to prioritize his relational energy in an intentional way.[8] His first relational priority was growing in his intimate friendship with his Father in heaven through the Holy Spirit (Matt 3:13–17). But looking at Jesus' earthly relationships, we see Jesus strategically prioritizing relationships. In Dunbar's language:

(1) Jesus had an *intimate friend* ("the beloved," John 21:20);

(2) three especially *close friends* (Matt 17:1; Mark 5:37; 13:3; 14:33);

(3) a group of *best friends* including Mary Magdalene (John 20:11–18), Mary, Lazarus, and Martha (John 11:1–44), and the other twelve disciples (Matt 12:1–4);

(4) a larger group of *good friends* ("the seventy," Luke 10:2);

(5) an even larger group of *friends* including Nicodemus, Joseph of Arimathea and the 120 (John 19:38–39; Acts 1:15);

---

8   Countless students of Scripture have commented on Jesus' prioritizing of relationships. I first remember learning about it from Issler, *Wasting Time With God*, 57–58. Until recently, I thought of Jesus' relational prioritization as concentric circles (as illustrated by Dunbar's circles of intimacy). A chapel message at Taylor University (February 15, 2021) by Kathy Chamberlain suggested a relationship pyramid which may be more helpful pastorally, and I have adapted her idea as presented here.

(6) a group of some five hundred *acquaintances* whom Paul describes as "sisters and brothers" to whom Jesus appeared after his resurrection (1 Cor 15:6);

(7) and then many more *known names* whom Jesus knew from his ministry to the crowds (Mark 3:32; 6:34; 8:2; 9:15; 10:46).

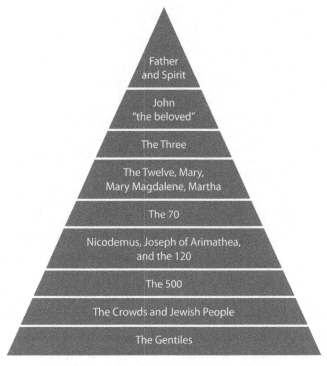

Figure 2: Jesus' Pyramid of Prioritized Friendship

Jesus' relational pyramid provides a model to follow, yet our lives look different today than the life he lived as a first century Jew and as one called to save humanity and redeem creation. While it is important to acknowledge these differences, there is still much about Jesus' life we are called to imitate (John 15:13; 1 Pet 2:21; 1 Cor 11:1; Eph 5:1; 1 Thess 1:6). If we take Jesus' pyramid of prioritized friendships as an example, what might a modified version look like today?

Figure 3: A Simplified Pyramid of Prioritized Friendship

Figure 3, "a simplified pyramid of prioritized friendship," provides one model of a modified version of Jesus' relational priorities for his disciples today. First, the top of the pyramid is friendship with the Father, the Spirit and the resurrected Jesus.[9] It is our personal friendship with Jesus of Nazareth that opens the door to friendship with our Father and the Spirit. For evangelicals, friendship with Jesus is a first

---

9   For more on being Jesus' friend see Oliver O'Donovan, *Entering into Rest*, Ethics as Theology 3 (Grand Rapids, MI: Eerdmans, 2017), 153–62.

priority, and while we are a trinitarian people, we are more accurately described as "Christocentric-Trinitarian."[10]

Second, the idea of "covenantal friends" has implications for both married and single followers of Christ. For those who are married, we are invited to be spiritual friends with our spouse. Aelred's opening line in *Spiritual Friendship*, "Here we are, you and I, and I hope that Christ makes a third with us," (1.1) applies not only to same-sex friendships, but also to all Christian marriages. Flourishing Christian marriages work to remain mindful of the loving presence of Christ within their home. The spouses recognize that their spiritual friendship gladly includes Jesus as a mutual third friend.

But we also must recognize that deeply committed friendships are not limited to Christian marriage. In the Bible we find examples of highly committed same-sex friendships between friends like David and Jonathan, Ruth and Naomi, and Jesus and the Apostle John. In addition to Aelred's examples, countless more recent examples of close male friendships could be cited including Dietrich Bonhoeffer and Eberhard Bethge or Sir John Finch and Sir Thomas Baines among many others.[11] Of the many examples of female friendship from the history of the church, consider the three-decade long friendship between Henrietta Mears and Charlotte Atwater.[12] Mears' friendship

---

10 For more on God's people as "Christocentric-Trinitarian" see: Uche Anizor and Hank Voss, *Representing Christ: A Vision for the Priesthood of All Believers* (Downers Grove, IL: IVP Academic, 2016), 88–103.

11 See further Wesley Hill, *Spiritual Friendship: Finding Love in the Church as a Celibate Gay Christian* (Grand Rapids, MI: Brazos, 2015).

12 Andrea Van Boven, *A Little Drop of Love: Henrietta Mears, How She Helped Change a Generation and You Can Too* (Eugene, OR: Wipf and Stock, 2020), 117–20.

with Atwater provided important support as she mentored the founders of over fifty ministries including Billy Graham (evangelist and founder of the Lausanne Movement), Bill and Vonette Bright (founders of Campus Crusade for Christ, now known as Cru), and Jim Rayborn (founder of Youth for Christ).[13] In centuries past a commitment to a lifelong friendship between two members of the same sex was known in both the eastern and western branches of Christianity. In the eastern church, a formal church service for solemnizing a lifelong commitment of friendship between people of the same sex was called "sibling-making" (*adelphopoiesis*).[14] In contrast with the more pagan practice of exchanging blood to become "blood-brothers," two friends would exchange crosses (usually worn around the neck) as a reminder of their friendship during a church service which included a special prayer of blessing over the friendship.

Today, contemporary North American culture has polluted friendship with the idea that almost any close friendship includes the possibility of sexual intimacy. In contrast, unmarried Christian men and women who choose to enter intentional, committed, same-sex spiritual friendship are committed to faithfully living in obedience to biblical teaching about sexual ethics.[15] The practice of committed same-sex friendships is a gift that the contemporary church needs to recover. In the context of spiritual friendship, these committed friendships represent a promise to pursue Christ together for a season

13 Henrietta C. Mears, *Dream Big: The Henrietta Mears Story*, ed. Earl Roe (Ventura, CA: Gospel Light, 2012), 3–10.

14 See especially Letter 11 on friendship and the related notes in Pavel Florensky, The Pillar and Ground of the Truth, trans. Boris Jakim (Princeton, NJ: Princeton University Press, 1997), 327–30.

15 Beth Felker Jones, *Faithful: A Theology of Sex* (Grand Rapids, MI: Zondervan, 2015).

or for life. Despite many wrong ideas about same-sex friendships today, Christian leaders must learn how to encourage, nurture, and bless these spiritual friendships within the church.[16]

Third, Figure 3 suggests all believers need an inner circle of trustworthy friends. This group includes Dunbar's categories of "close friends" (five to seven people) and "best friends" (twelve to fifteen people). Returning to Don Davis' *oikos* principle, we recall that these special relationships are gifts from God in need of wise stewardship. These relationships are worthy of our time, energy, and resources. Aelred's teaching encourages us that investing in these relationships develops our friendship skills, skills that then nurture and deepen our friendship with the Father, Son, and Holy Spirit.

Finally, we need to accept that friendships with Gospel coworkers, with believers, and with all peoples will be limited by our own finitude and by human fallenness. While it is not possible to be friends with everyone, we can still choose to be friendly to all. The people we meet on the bus or at a grocery store can be treated as potential friends. With Oliver O'Donovan, we choose to pursue an attitude of friendliness so as to say:

> I am not your friend, nor you mine, nor in this life are we ever likely to become friends; yet in God's eternity, and even in this life if it should so transpire, a friendship between us will be no bad thing.[17]

---

16 Michael K. Severe, "Annotated Bibliography: Sexual Orientation and Gender Identity Issues in Educational Ministry," *Christian Education Journal* 18, no. 2 (2021): 308–12.

17 O'Donovan, *Entering into Rest*, 145.

A careful listening to Aelred's *Spiritual Friendship*, as well as reflection on the biblical friendships of people like King David and King Jesus, reveal an essential principle of soul work and soul care. We can be loving neighbors to all, but not spiritual friends. Good spiritual stewardship of *oikos* networks requires conscious investment of time, energy, affections, and resources in selective relationships. When we choose to be intentional about our spiritual friendships, we follow Jesus' example of a way of life with varying levels of intentional relational investment.

In your journal, or on a piece of paper, pause now and identify your own pyramid of prioritized relationships. At what levels do you already have strong relationships? Where are areas that you hope to develop in this next year? Once our own pyramid of prioritized relationships is identified, how can spiritual friendships be nurtured into greater maturity? The next section will outline five practical skills that can help develop spiritual friendship.

Five Strategies for Building Spiritual Friendship

Christians today who hope to develop and deepen spiritual friendships have a wide variety of resources available to them in our shared sacred roots. In this section, we explore five tools for building spiritual friendships from the many used over the past twenty centuries.

Spiritual Friendship Deepened through Shared Spirituality

Aelred lived in the same place and followed the same rule of life for over four decades.[18] He and his friends

---

18 For an introduction and explanation of a rule of life see Hank Voss, "Soul Work and Soul Care: Learning to Be Intentional about Our 'Rule of Life,'" in Greg Peters, *Becoming a Community of Disciples*, 121–41.

were intentional about pursuing what Don Davis calls a "shared spirituality."[19] For Davis, a shared spirituality means practicing the same spiritual disciplines with spiritual friends regardless of whether we are alone or together. Aelred practiced shared spirituality with his community. His rhythm included four hours of daily prayer, reading, and meditation on God's word. All of the friends that he dialogues with in *Spiritual Friendship*— Ivo, Walter, and Gratian—shared this daily practice with him (along with all Benedictines). The four of them together with their whole community also held big parties (feasts) to celebrate things like Christ's birth (Christmas), Jesus' baptism and revelation to the world (Epiphany), Jesus' resurrection (Easter), and his ascension to the right hand of his Father (Ascension Day). They also set times to fast together, like the forty days of the season of the cross (Lent) or the time of waiting for Jesus' coming (Advent).

Today, spiritual friends can also benefit from practicing a shared spirituality. It could be as simple as setting regular times to pray while together or apart. It could include sharing a Bible reading plan. Reading through the Bible chronologically with friends can be strengthening both to friendship and to one's relationship with God. Many technological resources can make reading and sharing God's word with friends easier. Taking advantage of the Christian Year is another helpful way to deepen spiritual friendship. Even while apart, you can share fellowship with your friends knowing they are celebrating the same great events of salvation history (e.g. the birth, death, and resurrection of Jesus). As an example from the world of

---

19 Don Davis, *Sacred Roots: A Primer on Retrieving the Great Tradition* (Wichita, KS: The Urban Ministry Institute, 2010), 49–57, 103–15.

sports, observe how tens of millions of people "fellowship" each year through watching the Super Bowl or the World Cup, even though they are in many different locations. These fans are united by a "shared spirituality" of sorts. In addition to celebrating, spiritual friends also fast together, setting aside particular days of the week or year for practicing this discipline. Many churches fast for the first twenty-one days of the calendar year. Others choose to fast for the forty days leading up to Easter (Lent). There are many options, but learning to practice spiritual disciplines with spiritual friends is a wonderful way to deepen spiritual friendship.

Spiritual Friendship Deepened through Conversations

When Aelred decided he wanted to teach his community about spiritual friendship, he chose to write three conversations between friends about friendship. Aelred's book is built upon a long history of believers who intentionally set aside time for godly conversations with their friends. Consider four examples.

(1) The book of Job provides an example of friends holding regular and extensive spiritual conversations, conversations that are brutally honest. Even though Job's friends were not offering helpful input, the time they invested in their friendship with Job (e.g. sitting in silence for seven days) illustrates a deeper practice of friendship than many today.

(2) Aelred was influenced by a spiritual classic called *Conferences,* a book consisting of twenty-four conversations between Cassian (d. 435), his good

friend Germanus, and various spiritual mentors.
These conversations are still read by thousands of
believers every year with great spiritual reward.[20]

(3) Matteo Ricci (d. 1610), one of the first Christian
missionaries to China, believed deeply in the
importance of friendship and spiritual conversations
between friends. The first book he wrote in
Chinese was called, *On Friendship*, and it has
remained popular in China ever since.[21]

(4) The Puritans took spiritual conversations about God
and Scripture seriously.[22] They would often set times
to talk with one another about their souls and their
friendship with God. These conversations would
take place between friends, pastors and members
of their congregation, small groups of pastors,
husbands and wives, and parents and children.

Today, friends can practice the art of spiritual conversation
with just as much profit as previous generations. They can
set times to meet with friends for a walk or meal to talk
about the state of their souls, their mutual friendship with
Jesus, and things they are hearing in Scripture. Consider
setting regular times to talk with spiritual friends about
these matters. You could set a daily time (perhaps easiest
for families or those living together), a weekly time for

---

20 John Cassian, *John Cassian: The Conferences*, ed. Boniface Ramsey, Ancient
Christian Writers 57 (New York: Paulist, 1997); See also Cassian, *Institutes and
Conferences* in the Nicene and Post-Nicene Fathers.

21 Matteo Ricci, *On Friendship: One Hundred Maxims for a Chinese Prince*, trans.
Timothy Billings, (New York: Columbia University Press, 2009 [orig. 1595]).

22 Joanne J. Jung, *The Lost Discipline of Conversation: Surprising Lessons in Spiritual
Formation Drawn from the English Puritans* (Grand Rapids, MI: Zondervan, 2018).

a walk or a phone date, a monthly or even annual time to connect with a friend. You might consider creating a group at church that can help to form and deepen spiritual friendships through conversation and service. The Siafu Network is one example of how many churches among the poor are creating these spaces for spiritual friendship.[23]

Hopefully reading *Spiritual Friendship* has provided opportunity to talk with friends about spiritual friendship. Did you find these conversations helpful? If so, perhaps you can commit to reading and discussing another spiritual classic together? In sum, spiritual friends talk with one another about their souls and their pursuit of God as a regular component of their friendship.

Spiritual Friendship Deepened through Letter Writing

In *Letters of Faith through the Seasons*, James Houston makes a number of intriguing observations about letter writing.[24] He emphasizes that writing letters is a way to develop and deepen a culture of friendship. He notes that twenty-one of the twenty-nine New Testament books are actually letters to individuals or groups, and that some have described the whole Bible as God's love letter to us (e.g. Søren Kierkegaard). Houston also observes that throughout church history letter writing has remained an important ministry. To this day, we have over nine thousand letters preserved from the early centuries of the church. Among these many letters we find a long

---

23 Don L. Davis, *The SIAFU Network Guidebook: Standing Together for Christ in the City* (Wichita, KS: TUMI Press, 2013).

24 James Houston, *Letters of Faith Through the Seasons: December to May* (Vancouver, BC: Regent College, 2018).

tradition of sisters and brothers writing to one another to encourage each other in their walk with God. There are many examples of friends of the same sex, like Jerome and Augustine, who wrote long and thoughtful letters to one another.[25] But there are also many examples of friends of the opposite sex, like Jeanne Guyon and Bishop Fenelon, who were not married to one another, and yet who developed a deeply intimate spiritual friendship.[26]

More recently, Caroline Macdonald (d.1931) maintained a twenty-five-year ministry of friendship in Japan. A foundational theological principle in her philosophy of ministry was that "God is friend."[27] This principle led her to become friends with thousands of Japanese prisoners. As a result of these friendships, she became an influential voice calling for the reform of prisons in Japan. She also recognized that writing letters to friends was a central activity in her ministry. During her life she wrote thousands of letters of encouragement and exhortation to her incarcerated friends.

Today the practice of letter writing may seem out of date. But those willing to explore this tool will find it a reliable aid in sustaining and deepening spiritual friendships. Consider adapting or using this tool with spiritual friends. Perhaps you will commit to writing a letter of encouragement to a friend on his or her birthday?

---

25 Saint Jerome and Saint Augustine of Hippo, *The Correspondence (394–419), Between Jerome and Augustine of Hippo*, ed. Carolinne White, Studies in the Bible and Early Christianity 23 (Lewiston, NY: Mellen, 1990).

26 Madame Jeanne Guyon, *Letters of Jeanne Guyon*, trans. P. L. Upham, Reprint. (New Kensington, PA: Whitaker, 2013 [orig. 1870]).

27 Dana L. Robert, *Faithful Friendships: Embracing Diversity in Christian Community* (Grand Rapids: Eerdmans, 2019), 56–64.

Could you send a thoughtful digital communication (voice or video) with words of encouragement or exhortation? Will you decide to use sabbath or spiritual retreat days to write a regular letter to a spiritual friend or a group of friends? You might even consider writing a letter to a friend describing what you are learning about spiritual friendship as a result of reading this book.

Spiritual Friendship Deepened through Christian Marriage

On March 22, 1758, Jonathan Edwards died at the relatively young age of fifty-four. Shortly before he died, he wrote a final letter to his wife, Sarah. In it he encouraged her with these words, "the uncommon union, which has so long subsisted between us, has been of such a nature, as I trust is spiritual, and therefore will continue forever."[28] It is not likely that Edwards had read Aelred's *Spiritual Friendship*, but he came to a similar conclusion about the eternal nature of friendships rooted in Christ. Early in his first conversation about friendship, Aelred concludes that "friendship is eternal, provided it is true friendship" (1.21). Edwards' letter to his wife is an example of an eternal spiritual friendship that was nurtured from the time Sarah was thirteen years old.[29]

Married Christians are called to nurture a spiritual friendship with one another. Paul Stevens explains that while Aelred wrote his spiritual classic for same-sex friends,

---

28 George M. Marsden, *Jonathan Edwards: A Life* (New York: Yale University Press, 2003), 494.

29 Ibid., 93–94.

> his thoughts have a direct application to marriage. Aelred
> says that friendship in Christ is a direct path to God, not
> a diversion from God. . . . His thoughts about friendship
> have great relevance to married friends desiring a deeper
> relationship through spiritual conversation.[30]

Imagine a Christian community where all the husbands
and wives viewed their marriage as "a direct path to God,
not a diversion from God." What if they approached their
marriage as an eternal friendship, one Aelred describes
as "formed in Christ, advanced according to Christ, and
perfected by Christ" (1.10). Married believers have
a wonderful opportunity to pursue spiritual friendship
with one another. Aelred's *Spiritual Friendship* can offer
much practical help for spouses interested in pursuing
a deepened spiritual friendship together with Christ.

Spiritual Friendship Deepened through Eulogies

Before writing *Spiritual Friendship*, Aelred wrote a book
about love in response to a request from his good friend
Bernard of Clairvaux. In it, Aelred pauses to lament the
death of his good friend, Simon. The lament runs thirteen
pages in English translation, and at one-point Aelred writes:

> You are astonished that I am weeping; you are still
> more astonished that I go on living! For who would not
> be astonished that Aelred goes on living without Simon,
> except someone who does not know how sweet it was
> to live together, how sweet it would be to return together
> to the fatherland. So bear patiently with my tears, my
> sighs, the moaning of my heart, then.[31]

---

30 R. Paul Stevens, *Marriage Spirituality: Ten Disciplines for Couples Who Love God*, Reprint edition (Vancouver, BC: Regent College Publishing, 1997), 42.

31 *Mirror of Charity*, 1.98–114. Aelred of Rievaulx, *The Mirror of Charity*, trans. Elizabeth Connor, Cistercian Fathers 17 (Kalamazoo, MI: Cistercian, 1990), 148.

Aelred's eulogy testifies both to the good character of his friend Simon, and to the intimate spiritual friendship they enjoyed. It also points to a lost tool for developing a Christian community's understanding and vision for spiritual friendship. For many centuries, it was common for good friends to give a long eulogy about their friend when they died. For example, Gregory of Nazianzus' (d. 390) eulogy for his friend Bishop Basil (d. 379) runs seventy-three pages in its English translation.[32] Brian McGuire would go so far as to say that if a history of friendship was to be written, it would perhaps best be done by studying friends' laments after a friend's death.[33]

Leaders are often challenged to "begin with the end in mind." Why not start thinking now about the (temporary) end of a spiritual friendship by writing a eulogy for a friend? If your closest spiritual friend were to die today, what would you say about them and the nature of your spiritual friendship? Or think about what your vision might be for a spiritual friendship that lasted three or four decades or more. What do you hope that spiritual friendship would look like? Use your imagination to write a lament that describes your vision of the kind of friendship you hope to have with a spiritual friend at the end of your life. You don't need to wait for your friend to die to share this "eulogy." Why not turn it into a letter, and send it to your friend to share the reasons you appreciate them and your shared spiritual friendship?

---

32 Saint Gregory of Nazianzus, "On Basil the Great," in *Funeral Orations*, trans. Leo P. McCauley, vol. 22, Fathers of the Church (Washington: Catholic University of America Press, 1968), 27–99.

33 Brian Patrick McGuire, *Friendship and Community: The Monastic Experience, 350–1250* (Kalamazoo, MI: Cistercian, 1988), xvi.

Human limitations prevent us from writing eulogies for all friends, but perhaps thinking about a eulogy for one or two spiritual friends would be a way to deepen your spiritual friendship.

A Final Word about Developing Spiritual Friendships as a Spiritual Discipline

This soul work and soul care appendix provides one answer to the question, "so what?" How do we take Aelred's teaching about spiritual friendship and develop our own spiritual friendships? It began with a discussion of the importance of Christian leaders learning to intentionally become good stewards of their *oikos* circles of relationship, and then looked at King David and King Jesus as examples of biblical leaders who practiced a prioritized pyramid of relational investment. Neither David nor Jesus treated all around them equally when it came to intimate friendship. They recognized that good spiritual stewardship of *oikos* networks leads leaders to consciously invest their time, energy, affections, and resources in a small and selective set of prioritized relationships.

Like all spiritual disciplines, it is important to remember that the activity of spiritual friendship does not earn us a more intimate relationship with God. Rather, the spiritual discipline postures us so as to receive God's grace and self-revelation in increased measure.[34] Ultimately, growth in our relationship with the Father, Son, and Holy Spirit is a gift of grace.

---

34 "God has ordained the disciplines of the spiritual life as the means by which we place ourselves where he can bless us" (Richard J. Foster, *Celebration of Discipline: The Path to Spiritual Growth* [San Francisco: Harper, 1998], 7).

Once we recognize the need to invest time and energy into relationships with people we trust to guard our souls, then we need practical and proven strategies to practice spiritual friendship as a spiritual discipline. Five strategies were suggested above, and these five are not the only ones available. Whatever strategy you use, remember two things. First, spiritual friendship is a gift from God, and it must be received as a gift. Second, begin now to be intentional about pursuing spiritual friendships with people in your *oikos* circles.

Be warned, however, that the pursuit of spiritual friendship is like any good gift from God; it can be twisted by the world, the flesh, and the Devil. Some Christian communities considered Aelred's teaching on the nurturing of spiritual friendship to be so dangerous that they banned his book.[35] Consider these four potential dangers. First, spiritual friendships are always in danger of becoming self-focused instead of Christ-focused. When they fall to this temptation they become possessive, exclusive and unhealthy in various ways.

A second example can be seen in both the classical and Christian traditions where many thought it either impossible or too dangerous, for men and women to be friends. Some, with a slightly more positive view, suggest that only married men and women can be friends, but beyond the marriage covenant, no cross-sex friendships are possible. Aelred would disagree with both of these fear-based approaches to Christian friendship between the sexes, pointing to the many examples from Christian history of men and women who had healthy and beautiful spiritual friendships

---

35 McGuire, *Friendship & Community*, 331.

(1.29). More recently, Henry Clay Trumbull (great grandfather of Elizabeth Elliot) has provided dozens of examples of friendship between the sexes in a chapter entitled "Who Can Be Friends?"[36] Certainly friendship between the sexes can present dangers in the highly sexualized culture prevalent today, but abuses should not be used as an excuse to prevent deep friendships between sisters and brothers in the family of God. If you do not have spiritual friends of the opposite sex, take some time to consider how your life might look different if you opened yourself to a broader understanding of friendship within the kingdom of God.

While some focus on the danger of friendship between the sexes, others find danger in the opposite direction. For those with same-sex attraction, who aim to live faithfully to traditional biblical teaching about sexuality, the practice of building same-sex friendships can feel difficult or even impossible. How does one become friends with a member of the same sex without falling into some kind of sexual temptation? Similar to friendship between the sexes, deep and eternal friendship within the body of Christ is possible for those who experience same-sex attraction.[37]

A fourth set of dangers often appears when two individuals seek to build a spiritual friendship across chasms of class, culture, race or significant power differentials without recognizing the differences in lived realities that shape

---

36 Henry Clay Trumbull, *Friendship the Master-Passion: Or, The Nature and History of Friendship, and Its Place as a Force in the World* (New York: Charles Scribner, 1912), 105–14.

37 See the frank discussions of this challenge in Wesley Hill, *Spiritual Friendship: Finding Love in the Church as a Celibate Gay Christian* (Ada, MI: Brazos, 2015).

their experiences and perceptions.[38] While many in the
world despair that these kinds of friendships are possible,
Scripture and the testimony of believers from previous
generations offers hope. Aelred discusses the challenge of
being a friend to those to whom he is both "boss" and
pastor (3.114–118). His stories and example show that it
is possible for a pastor and members of the congregation
to be deep spiritual friends (3.119–127). A more recent
example is described by John Perkins, an African American
pastor and community leader, who became friends with
Tommy Tarrants. Tommy was a former Ku Klux Klan
member responsible for bombing many churches and
synagogues, but who eventually came to know the
forgiveness and grace of Jesus. After describing their
current friendship, Perkins asks, "Why would we want
to go to heaven where every tribe and every tongue will
be worshiping together at the feet of our God if we don't
want to be friends with everyone [all cultures] now?"[39]

If you have persevered this far, you are well equipped to
continue the journey of spiritual friendship. The pursuit
of spiritual friendship is not without danger, but it is a
reliable means of grace whereby we are drawn into greater
friendship with the triune God. Those who have studied
the art of friendship know that the friend of my friend is
also my friend. For believers who are friends with Jesus,
we have also received the wonderful privilege of meeting
his spiritual friends from every culture and generation.
Dana Robert is correct when she writes, "Friendship with

---

38 Robert, *Faithful Friendships*, 188–90.

39 John M. Perkins and Karen Waddles, *He Calls Me Friend: The Healing Power of Friendship in a Lonely World* (Chicago: Moody, 2019), 138–39.

Jesus, and with others through him, is a core value of Christian identity and practice."[40] May you find much joy as the Holy Spirit leads you to discover and deepen your friendships with Jesus and his eternal friends.

---

40 Robert, *Faithful Friendships*, 12.

Continuing the Conversation

I have placed *** next to those resources I think especially helpful. For overviews of Aelred's life and additional insight into *Spiritual Friendship* see:

Aelred of Rievaulx: Spiritual Friendship. Edited by Marsha L. Dutton. Translated by Lawrence C. Braceland. Collegeville, MN: Cistercian, 2010.***

Spiritual Friendship: The Classic Text with a Spiritual Commentary by Dennis Billy, C.Ss.R. Translated by M. Eugenia Laker. Notre Dame, IN: Ave Maria, 2008.

Aelred of Rievaulx's Spiritual Friendship. Translated by Mark F. Williams. Scranton, PA: University of Scranton Press, 2002.

Bernard of Clairvaux and Aelred of Rievaulx. *The Love of God and Spiritual Friendship.* Edited by James M. Houston. Abridged. Portland, OR: Multnomah, 1983.***

Dutton, Marsha, ed. *A Companion to Aelred of Rievaulx (1110–1167).* Brill's Companions to the Christian Tradition 76. Leiden: Brill, 2016.

For deeper explorations on the importance of Spiritual Friendship in the lives of Christian leaders and in relation to particular topics see:

Austin, Victor Lee. *Friendship: The Heart of Being Human.* Pastoring for Life. Grand Rapids: Baker Academic, 2020.***

Carmichael, Liz. *Friendship: Interpreting Christian Love, a History of the Interpretation of "Agape" as Friendship-Love in the Western Christian Tradition.* London: T&T Clark, 2004.

Fernando, Ajith. *Reclaiming Friendship: Relating to Each Other in a Frenzied World.* Scottdale, PA: Herald, 1993.***

Hill, Wesley. *Spiritual Friendship: Finding Love in the Church as a Celibate Gay Christian.* Grand Rapids, Michigan: Brazos Press, 2015.***

Issler, Klaus. *Wasting Time With God: A Christian Spirituality of Friendship With God.* Downers Grove: IVP, 2001.

Lewis, C. S. *The Four Loves.* London: Geoffrey Bles, 1960.***

Nouwen, Henri. *Adam: God's Beloved.* Maryknoll, NY: Orbis, 1997.

Perkins, John M., and Karen Waddles. *He Calls Me Friend: The Healing Power of Friendship in a Lonely World.* Chicago: Moody, 2019.

Robert, Dana L. *Faithful Friendships: Embracing Diversity in Christian Community.* Grand Rapids: Eerdmans, 2019.

Stevens, R. Paul. *Marriage Spirituality: Ten Disciplines for Couples Who Love God.* Regent College Publishing, 1989.

White, Carolinne. *Christian Friendship in the Fourth Century.* New York: Cambridge University Press, 1992.

Map of Important Places

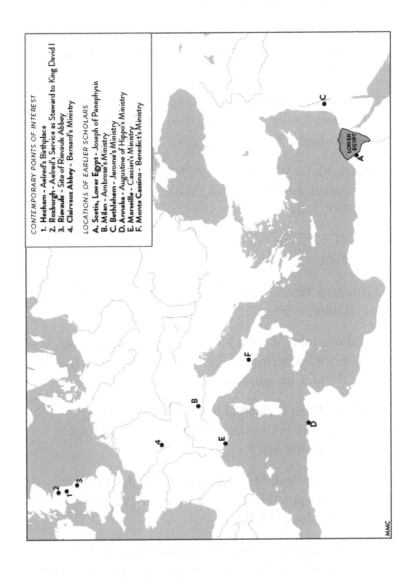

CONTEMPORARY POINTS OF INTEREST

1. Hexham - Aelred's Birthplace
2. Roxburgh - Aelred's Service as Steward to King David I
3. Rievaulx - Site of Rievaulx Abbey
4. Clairvaux Abbey - Bernard's Ministry

LOCATIONS OF EARLIER SCHOLARS

A. Scetis, Lower Egypt - Joseph of Panephysis
B. Milan - Ambrose's Ministry
C. Bethlehem - Jerome's Ministry
D. Annaba - Augustine of Hippo's Ministry
E. Marseille - Cassian's Ministry
F. Monte Cassino - Benedict's Ministry

LOWER EGYPT

MMC

A Letter to God's Friends and Fellow Warriors On Why We Read the Sacred Roots Spiritual Classics Together

---

Scholars like big books; small books change the world.

~ Rev. Dr. Glen Scorgie

Dear Friends and Fellow Warriors,

Greetings in the strong name of Jesus! What a joy to know that Jesus calls us "Friend" (John 15). What an honor to stand with sisters and brothers from every century and culture to shout, "Worthy is the Lamb!" What a privilege to serve in the Lamb's army, not fighting flesh and blood, but God's *internal* (the flesh), *external* (the world) and *infernal* (the Devil) enemies. In light of this cosmic struggle, we put on a wartime (not peacetime) mindset as we follow Jesus. Moses stated that God is present and at work in every generation (Ps 90:1), and the Sacred Roots Spiritual Classics are for those who desire to be used within their sphere of influence like David was used by God in his generation (Ps 57:2; Acts 13:36).

Our Context: A Battle with God's Internal, External, and Infernal Enemies

Scripture teaches our daily need to choose a missional mindset (Matt 6:10). God's kingdom never advances in neutral territory. Every inch in creation, including each inch of our soul, is a contested battlefield. God's enemies are threefold. First, there is an *internal* enemy hiding within the heart of each redeemed child of God. God loves us, even though we often battle a "Judas-heart"—a tendency to betray our Lord (John 12:6). Scripture names this brokenness the "flesh," the old "man" or the "sin nature" (Rom 8; Gal 5–6). We work to kill ("mortify") this sin lest it succeed in killing us (Rom 8:13).

Second, as followers of Jesus, we battle all *external* enemies opposing the Lamb's kingdom. Sickened by sin, polluted by greed, corrupted by self-centeredness, idolatry and oppression; our world is not the way it is supposed to be. What God created good has been twisted and now often grieves the Holy Spirit. We choose to stand with Shadrach, Meshach and Abednego in refusing to bow to the principalities and powers of the age (Dan 3), or to accept the besetting sins of our ethnicities, nations and generations. Scripture and our sacred roots shine painful yet purifying light on our blind spots.

Finally, we are not ignorant of the Devil's schemes. We may not know if a demon's name is "Screwtape" or "Legion," but we do know that an *infernal* enemy opposes God's kingdom *shalom*. He is the Devil, Satan, the Father of Lies, the Accuser, and one day soon he and his demons will be completely crushed. In this time between the times, the Lamb's followers resist and renounce the Devil and all his ways with the sword of the Spirit which is the Word of God.

Our Mission: To Be Faithful Stewards and Wise Servants in Our Generation

Scripture contains a number of "history" psalms (Pss 78, 105, 106, 136; Neh 9:6–38; cf. Heb 11). These songs challenge us to reflect on women and men who chose to serve God in their generation—Abraham and Sarah,

Moses, Phinehas, Rahab, David, Esther and many others. History psalms also warn of those who ignored or refused to participate in God's work (Pharaoh, Dathan, Abiram, Og). Leaders like Rahab the prostitute (Matt 1:5; Heb 11:35; Jas 2:25) and King David were far from perfect (Ps 51). Yet Scripture declares that leaders like David "served the purposes of God in his own generation" (Acts 13:36).

Do you want God to use you in your generation? Are you willing to be a David or Esther today? God is already at work in our communities, schools and workplaces. Sometimes the neighborhoods with the greatest challenges (those with giants like "Goliath" and armies of Philistine enemies) are the very places God finds servants and stewards he can use (1 Sam 17; 1 Cor 4:1).

Like King David, Prince Kaboo of the Kru people in Liberia chose to participate in God's work in his generation. As a child, Prince Kaboo (1873–1893) was taken hostage by a rival tribe and was about to be executed when he experienced a supernatural deliverance. After weeks of traveling through the jungle, Kaboo arrived at a mission station near Monrovia, Liberia's capital. There, as a fourteen-year-old teenager, he wholeheartedly gave his life to Jesus Christ.

Prince Kaboo took on the name Samuel Kaboo Morris at his baptism, and he spent the next four years working and

studying Scripture—especially Jesus' teaching about the
Holy Spirit as recorded by his friend John (John 14–17).
Kaboo was fascinated with the Holy Spirit, for he had
personally experienced the Holy Spirit's powerful
deliverance. Eventually, the missionaries told Kaboo they
had taught him all they knew and that if he wanted to
learn more about the Holy Spirit, he would need to travel
to the United States. Kaboo felt the need for more training
about the Holy Spirit before being ready to return to the
Kru as an evangelist. With no shoes or money, Kaboo
walked to Monrovia's harbor to find passage to New York—
trusting his Father in Heaven to provide.

Kaboo's story is powerful. The ship that transported
Kaboo experienced revival with the captain and many
crew coming to Christ. Within a few hours of arriving
in New York, Kaboo led seventeen men to Christ at an
inner-city rescue mission. On his third day in the United
States, the eighteen-year-old evangelist preached at a
Sunday school meeting and revival broke out with a new
missionary society organized that very day. God provided
money for Kaboo's college tuition, housing, books and
necessities. By the end of his first week in America,
Kaboo had arrived in Fort Wayne, Indiana to begin
studying at Taylor University—an evangelical college
committed to raising up workers for the harvest fields
who walk in the power of the Holy Spirit (Matt 9:36;
Acts 1:8).

Prince Kaboo's arrival at Taylor University transformed
not only Taylor University's campus, but also the whole
city of Fort Wayne. On his first Sunday in town, Kaboo
walked to the front of the church and asked for permission
to pray. As he prayed, the power and presence of the Holy

Spirit descended on the congregation in a way none had ever experienced before. The pastor reported, "what I said and what Sammy said I do not remember, but I know my soul was on fire as never before. . . . No such visitation of the Holy Spirit had ever been witnessed" by our congregation.[1]

Two years later, on May 12, 1893, at the age of twenty, Prince Samuel Kaboo Morris died from an illness contracted after traveling through a snowstorm to preach. Since his death, Kaboo's story has influenced thousands of students at Taylor University and elsewhere to participate with the Holy Spirit in mission and seek the Spirit's power in witness. John Wengatz was a student at Taylor in 1906, the year he first read Kaboo's story. Some fifty years later, after a lifetime invested as a missionary in Africa, Wengatz remarked "my tears never cease to flow as I read that unrepeatable story."[2] Although Kaboo died at twenty, he was used mightily by God in his generation. Will those who tell the story of your life say the same?

Our Vision: Toward Ten Thousand "Tozers"

If you are pursuing God with the same passion and hunger displayed by Samuel Kaboo Morris, than you will be glad to meet A. W. Tozer (1897–1963). Tozer grew up poor without the opportunity to complete high school. While working in a tire factory he heard the good news

---

1   Lindley Baldwin, *Samuel Morris: The African Boy God Sent to Prepare an American University for Its Mission to the World* (Minneapolis, MN: Bethany House, 1987), 59.

2   John Wengatz, *Sammy Morris: Spirit-Filled Life* (Upland, IN: Taylor University Press, 1954), Preface.

about Jesus, repented and believed. At nineteen, he began
to preach, becoming one of the most influential pastors
in his generation. His books *The Pursuit of God* and *The
Knowledge of the Holy* have helped millions know and
love the Triune God revealed in Scripture. When asked
how he learned to read Scripture with such clarity and
theological depth, Pastor Tozer would often point to his
"friends" and "teachers." These teachers were a list of
some thirty-five Christian spiritual classics read and reread
throughout Tozer's life. Sacred Roots Spiritual Classics
(SRSC) are for those with a hunger for the Holy Spirit like
Prince Kaboo and a desire to be used like Pastor Tozer.

The Sacred Roots Project envisions ten thousand
Christian leaders, serving in challenging ministry contexts
across North America, engaging with spiritual classics
in community by the year 2030. Will you join this growing
community as we pursue God together by reading and
discussing spiritual classics with gospel friends and
kingdom coworkers (Matt 9:35)?

A larger dream also informs the Sacred Roots Project—a
dream that imagines a million Christian workers equipped
to serve among the global poor (Matt 9:36–38). The
Center for the Study of Global Christianity reports that
in the middle of 2020 there are approximately two and
a half billion people living in urban poverty.[3] This number
will increase to over four billion by the year 2050. Sacred
Roots dreams of equipping one million Christian leaders
among this great multitude—women and men like Prince
Kaboo—with access to excellent editions of some of the
greatest spiritual classics the Christian tradition has

---

3   For the most current statistics, see www.gordonconwell.edu/center-for-global-christianity/resources/status-of-global-christianity/.

produced. Ultimately, the goal is increased faithfulness as leaders mature in representing Christ in local churches that are centered on Scripture, grounded in Great Tradition truth (Nicene), and engaged in contextually relevant witness to Christ's love in thousands of diverse contexts.[4]

Our Strategy:
Scripture, Friendship and Spiritual Classics

Sacred Roots' strategy is simple. We believe fresh readings of Christian spiritual classics can lead Christian leaders into a deeper engagement with the God revealed in Scripture and into deeper friendships with one another.

Christian spiritual classics strengthen and deepen our roots in Scripture and help us produce the Spirit's fruit. One day Jesus asked a serious student of the Bible a simple question, *"How do you read it?"* (Luke 10:26). Of the more than three hundred questions asked by Jesus in the Gospels, few are more relevant today. Faithfulness in our generation demands that we learn to read Scripture in a way consistent with the foundational truths held by followers of Jesus in every culture since the first century. We read Christian spiritual classics to discover faithful and fruitful readings of Scripture. As Dr. Davis has noted, the church's "Great Tradition" perennially opens our eyes to new riches in Scripture's "Authoritative Tradition."[5]

A truth believed by all Christians, in all places, and at all times is that there is one God who exists as Father, Son, and Holy Spirit. From "before to beyond time," an eternal

---

4   Don Davis, *Sacred Roots: A Primer on Retrieving the Great Tradition* (Wichita, KS: The Urban Ministry Institute, 2010), 35–45.

5   Ibid.

friendship between the Trinity's three persons has existed at the center of reality. Spiritual friendship provides the start and heart of truth. Just as spiritual classics can reveal new riches from Scripture, so they help us grow in love for God and neighbors. They can provide practical help in deepening our friendships with the Father, the Son, the Holy Spirit and with other believers—both with believers in this generation and with those surrounding us in the great cloud of witnesses (Heb 12:1; 13:7). Why do Christian leaders desperately need to pursue strong friendships? Start with these three reasons.

1. First, each of us has eyes far too small to see what God wants to show us! No one can begin to grasp the great things God is doing across 100 billion galaxies and throughout the many generations since the universe's creation. Friends, standing in different places provides additional eyes to see from different perspectives what God is doing in the world and across history.

2. Second, each of us battles a sinful nature that distorts our perception of the truth. We need friends who speak truth to us, sharpening us like iron sharpening iron (Prov 27:17).

3. Third, all of us view creation through a particular culture's time and place. Each culture exists with a unique version of virtue and vice. Friends who speak to us from other cultures and centuries often affirm virtues in our culture, but they can also reflect ways our culture's vice habitually offends against kingdom *shalom*.

In sum, Sacred Roots Spiritual Classics help us grow in our friendship with God and neighbor (Matt 22:37–40). Neighbors include the living Christian leaders with whom we read and discuss this spiritual classic. However, "neighbor" also includes the author (or authors) of this spiritual classic. These women and men walked faithfully with God and neighbor. Their life and teachings produced good fruit in their generation and then continued to do so in the lives of other Christian leaders—often across many cultures and centuries. As an editorial team, we can personally testify to the fruitfulness of the time we have spent with our "friends," the "ancient witnesses" in the Sacred Roots Spiritual Classics. If you choose to invest in careful conversation with these saints of old (Heb 13:7), we are confident you will not only experience practical fruit in the present, but you will also gain new friends for eternity.

Tactical Notes: Christian Leaders Are Christian Readers

Throughout church history, fruitful Christian leaders have been intentional readers. Augustine (d. 430), a pastor and bishop in Africa, was challenged to a new level of ministry by reading a spiritual biography about an Egyptian Christian leader named Anthony (d. 356).[6] Protestant leaders like Martin Luther, John Calvin, John Wesley, Elizabeth Fry, Phoebe Palmer and many others all published editions of spiritual classics for Christian leaders in their generation. Charles Harrison Mason (d. 1961), founder of the largest Pentecostal denomination in North America (Church of God in Christ), was called to ministry through a reading

---

6   Athanasius, *Renewal in Christ: Athanasius on the Christian Life*, ed. Jeremy Treat, Sacred Roots Spiritual Classics 6 (Wichita, KS: The Urban Ministry Institute, 2022).

of the autobiography of missionary and evangelist Amanda Smith.[7] More recently, leaders like C. S. Lewis, A. W. Tozer, James Houston, and Rick Warren have encouraged Christian leaders to read wisely, especially choosing Christian spiritual classics.[8]

How to Read the Text

Plan your reading. Reading a spiritual classic is a bit like reading your Bible. You can read it anywhere or anytime, but there are times and places that will position you to better receive insight and truth. SRSC readers tend to read each spiritual classic several times, and many will "read" it in both a written version (print or electronic) and in an audible version (audiobook). We read to hear what the original author of the text is saying and to understand what the Holy Spirit might be directing our attention to hear or reflect upon. On your day of rest (Sabbath) reserve some time to read or at least set aside some time to plan when you will read from your spiritual classic that week. If you have a daily commute, perhaps use some of the time to listen and reflect on an audible version of the SRSC.

Work your reading plan. Once you have planned to read your spiritual classic, begin with the Introduction. The introduction is written by a contemporary friend with significant ministry experience. This friend has spent much

---

7   Amanda Smith, *An Autobiography: The Story of the Lord's Dealings with Mrs. Amanda Smith, the Colored Evangelist; Containing an Account of Her Life Work of Faith, and Her Travels in America, England, Ireland, Scotland, India, and Africa, as an Independent Missionary* (Chicago: Meyer, 1893).

8   Explore the essays in Jamin Goggin and Kyle Strobel, eds., *Reading the Christian Spiritual Classics: A Guide for Evangelicals* (Downers Grove, IL: InterVarsity, 2013).

time reading and getting to know the spiritual classic and the author who wrote it. Often, the introduction is written by someone who has read the spiritual classic dozens, if not hundreds, of times. The introduction will help you get the most out of your first several readings of the text.

After reading the Introduction, notice that all Sacred Roots Spiritual Classics are divided into eight chapters. These chapters are not always of equal length, but they all are weighty enough to engage your head, heart, and hands as well as your habitat and habits. Following the eight chapters, every SRSC includes a short section called Continuing the Conversation. If you enjoyed reading the spiritual classic, then Continuing the Conversation will help you discover more resources to engage the author(s) of the spiritual classic.

The Sacred Roots Spiritual Classics are divided into ten parts to make it easier to talk about the text with friends and coworkers. The table below provides four (of many) examples of how to read a SRSC with a group of friends. When friends commit to read and discuss a SRSC together, the group is called a Sacred Roots Cohort.

SRSC Section to Read	"Sunday School" Class	"Church-Based Seminary" Module	Monthly Pastor's Meeting	Quarterly Retreat Discussion Group
	Ten Weeks	Eight Weeks	Monthly	Quarterly
Introduction	Week 1	Week 1	Month 1	Read text before retreat and then discuss
Ch. 1	Week 2		Month 1	
Ch. 2	Week 3	Week 2	Month 1	
Ch. 3	Week 4	Week 3	Month 2	
Ch. 4	Week 5	Week 4	Month 2	
Ch. 5	Week 6	Week 5	Month 2	
Ch. 6	Week 7	Week 6	Month 2	
Ch. 7	Week 8	Week 7	Month 3	
Ch. 8	Week 9	Week 8	Month 3	
Continuing the Conversation	Week 10	Week 8	Month 3	

Review your reading. The best readers, like the best leaders, do more than make a plan and work it. They also pause to take time to review their work—or in this case—their reading.[9] Robert Clinton has noted that only around 25 percent of leaders in the Bible finished well.[10] If we hope to finish well in our generation we must learn to *attend* to our habitat, our head, our heart, our hands, and our habits. To *attend* means to pay attention, to apply our self, to prioritize and to value something enough to give it our time and our energy. Each chapter concludes with five types of questions aimed at helping you review your progress toward finishing well and hearing Jesus say, "Well done, good and faithful servant" (Matt 25:23).

Habitat? *Habitat questions* ask us to pause and look around at our environment, our culture, our generation, our nationality, and the things that make up the *Zeitgeist* (spirit of the times). Questions may ask about the author's habitat or our own. Since the SRSC were written across many centuries and cultures, they often help us notice aspects of our culture needing attention.

Head? Auguste Rodin's sculpture known as *The Thinker* sits before an 18-foot-tall sculpture called *The Gates of Hell*. The massive sculptural group reflects Rodin's engagement with a spiritual classic by Dante, *The Divine Comedy*. *Head questions* require serious intellectual

---

9   The PWR (Plan, Work, Review) process is explained further by Don Allsman, *The Heroic Venture: A Parable of Project Leadership* (Wichita, KS: The Urban Ministry Institute, 2006).

10   Robert Clinton, *The Making of a Leader: Recognizing the Lessons and Stages of Leadership Development*, Rev. ed. (Colorado Springs, CO: NavPress, 2012), 185–87.

engagement as you talk with friends about the author's ideas, claims, and proposals.

 Heart? In August of 1541 John Calvin wrote a letter to a friend with this promise: "When I remember that I am not my own, I offer up my heart presented as a sacrifice to God." Calvin's personal seal expressed this sincere desire. God not only owns our mind, but also our will and emotions. *Heart questions* will help you attend to the people and things to which you give your loves.

 Hands? Albrecht Dürer sketched a drawing called *Study of the Hands of an Apostle* in the year 1508. The apostles were men of action, yet Dürer portrays the apostle's hands in prayer. The action to which SRSC call us are often surprising. *Hands questions* will challenge you to evaluate carefully what action you are to take after a particular reading.

 Habits? Charlotte Mason (d. 1923) was a master teacher. She believed Christian formation must carefully attend to habit formation. Like laying railroad tracks, habit formation is hard work. But once laid, great work requires little effort just as railroad cars run smoothly on tracks. *Habit questions* challenge you to reflect on small daily or weekly actions that form your character and the character of those around you.

Reading with Friends

The Sacred Roots Spiritual Classics are not meant to be read alone; indeed, it is impossible to do so. Every time we open a SRSC we read a book that *has been read* by thousands of Christian leaders in previous generations, *is being read* by thousands of Christian leaders in our generation, and *will be read* (if the return of Christ tarries) by thousands of Christian leaders in generations after us. The readers before us have already finished their race. These thousands of Christian leaders read the text in hundreds of different cultures and across dozens of different generations. All these "friends" read this text with you now. As you read the SRSC, imagine yourself talking about *Benedict's Rule* (SRSC 2) with the reformer Martin Luther; or picture yourself discussing Madam Guyon's *A Short and Easy Method of Prayer* with the missionary Amy Carmichael. Remember you never read a Sacred Roots Spiritual Classic alone.

However, it is not just leaders who have gone before, it is also leaders in the present with whom you must imagine reading this SRSC. Whatever benefit you find in reading will be doubled when you share it with a friend. Whatever trouble or difficulty you find in reading the text will be halved when you share it with a friend. Resolve to never read a Sacred Roots Spiritual Classic alone.

Perhaps you have noticed that the word "generation" has already appeared in this preface more than fifteen times? The SRSC represent the work of many generations working together. Five generations of evangelicals have worked and prayed together on this project since its public commencement in 2018. But these five generations of living evangelicals represent only a small sample of the many generations who have tested the faithfulness and fruitfulness of the SRSC. Why does this matter? In part, it matters because these texts are treasures to use and then pass on to the next generation of leaders. Recognize the emerging leaders God has called you to serve and steward—share the Sacred Roots Spiritual Classics with them.

Careful readers of Scripture know that the most influential leaders among God's people have always worked in teams. King David's teams became legends—"the three," "the thirty." The list of Paul's missionary and ministry team members whose first name we know from the New Testament runs to nearly one hundred. Our Sacred Roots team of teams prays that this text will be a blessing and a reliable resource for you and your gospel friends as you pursue kingdom business together.

Grace and Peace,

Don, Uche, Greg, May, Ryan, Isaiah, and Hank

The Nicene Creed with Scriptural Support

The Urban Ministry Institute

We believe in one God,
Deut 6:4–5; Mark 12:29; 1 Cor 8:6

the Father Almighty,
Gen 17:1; Dan 4:35; Matt 6:9; Eph 4:6; Rev 1:8

Maker of heaven and earth
Gen 1:1; Isa 40:28; Rev 10:6

and of all things visible and invisible.
Ps 148; Rom 11:36; Rev 4:11

We believe in one Lord Jesus Christ, the only Begotten Son
of God, begotten of the Father before all ages, God
from God, Light from Light, True God from True God,
begotten not created, of the same essence as the Father,
John 1:1–2; 3:18; 8:58; 14:9–10; 20:28; Col 1:15, 17; Heb 1:3–6

through whom all things were made.
John 1:3; Col 1:16

Who for us men and for our salvation came down from
heaven and was incarnate by the Holy Spirit and the
Virgin Mary and became human.
Matt 1:20–23; Luke 19:10; John 1:14; 6:38

Who for us too, was crucified under Pontius Pilate,
suffered and was buried.
Matt 27:1–2; Mark 15:24–39, 43–47; Acts 13:29; Rom 5:8;
Heb 2:10; 13:12

The third day he rose again according to the Scriptures,
Mark 16:5–7; Luke 24:6–8; Acts 1:3; Rom 6:9; 10:9; 2 Tim 2:8

ascended into heaven, and is seated at the right hand of the Father.
Mark 16:19; Eph 1:19–20

He will come again in glory to judge the living and the dead, and his Kingdom will have no end.
Isa 9:7; Matt 24:30; John 5:22; Acts 1:11; 17:31; Rom 14:9; 2 Cor 5:10; 2 Tim 4:1

We believe in the Holy Spirit, the Lord and life-giver,
Gen 1:1–2; Job 33:4; Pss 104:30; 139:7–8; Luke 4:18–19; John 3:5–6; Acts 1:1–2; 1 Cor 2:11; Rev 3:22

who proceeds from the Father and the Son,
John 14:16–18, 26; 15:26; 20:22

who together with the Father and Son is worshiped and glorified,
Isa 6:3; Matt 28:19; 2 Cor 13:14; Rev 4:8

who spoke by the prophets.
Num 11:29; Mic 3:8; Acts 2:17–18; 2 Pet 1:21

We believe in one holy, catholic, and apostolic Church.
Matt 16:18; 1 Cor 1:2; 10:17; Eph 5:25–28; 1 Tim 3:15; Rev 7:9

We acknowledge one baptism for the forgiveness of sin,
Acts 22:16; Eph 4:4–5; 1 Pet 3:21

And we look for the resurrection of the dead and the life of the age to come.
Isa 11:6–10; Mic 4:1–7; Luke 18:29–30; Rev 21:1–5; 21:22–22:5

Amen.

Memory Verses

Below are suggested memory verses, one for each section of the Creed.

The Father

Rev 4:11 (ESV) — Worthy are you, our Lord and God, to receive glory and honor and power, for you created all things, and by your will they existed and were created.

The Son

John 1:1 (ESV) — In the beginning was the Word, and the Word was with God, and the Word was God.

The Son's Mission

1 Cor 15:3–5 (ESV) — For what I received I passed on to you as of first importance: that Christ died for our sins according to the Scriptures, that he was buried, that he was raised on the third day according to the Scriptures, and that he appeared to Peter, and then to the Twelve.

The Holy Spirit

Rom 8:11 (ESV) — If the Spirit of him who raised Jesus from the dead dwells in you, he who raised Christ Jesus from the dead will also give life to your mortal bodies through his Spirit who dwells in you.

The Church

1 Pet 2:9 (ESV) — But you are a chosen race, a royal priesthood, a holy nation, a people for his own possession, that you may proclaim the excellencies of him who called you out of darkness into his marvelous light.

Our Hope

1 Thess 4:16–17 (ESV) — For the Lord himself will descend from heaven with a cry of command, with the voice of an archangel, and with the sound of the trumpet of God. And the dead in Christ will rise first. Then we who are alive, who are left, will be caught up together with them in the clouds to meet the Lord in the air, and so we will always be with the Lord.

From Before to Beyond Time:
The Plan of God and Human History
Adapted from Suzanne de Dietrich. *God's Unfolding Purpose.*
Philadelphia: Westminster Press, 1976.

I. Before Time (Eternity Past)

1 Cor. 2:7 (ESV) – But we impart a secret and hidden wisdom of God, which God decreed before the ages for our glory (cf. Titus 1:2).

A. The Eternal Triune God
B. God's Eternal Purpose
C. The Mystery of Iniquity
D. The Principalities and Powers

II. Beginning of Time (Creation and Fall)

Gen. 1:1 (ESV) – In the beginning, God created the heavens and the earth.

A. Creative Word
B. Humanity
C. Fall
D. Reign of Death and First Signs of Grace

III. Unfolding of Time (God's Plan Revealed through Israel)

Gal. 3:8 (ESV) – And the Scripture, foreseeing that God would justify the Gentiles by faith, preached the Gospel beforehand to Abraham, saying, "In you shall all the nations be blessed" (cf. Rom. 9:4-5).

A. Promise (Patriarchs)
B. Exodus and Covenant at Sinai
C. Promised Land
D. The City, the Temple, and the Throne (Prophet, Priest, and King)
E. Exile
F. Remnant

IV. Fullness of Time (Incarnation of the Messiah)

Gal. 4:4-5 (ESV) – But when the fullness of time had come, God sent forth his Son, born of woman, born under the law, to redeem those who were under the law, so that we might receive adoption as sons.

A. The King Comes to His Kingdom
B. The Present Reality of His Reign
C. The Secret of the Kingdom:
   the Already and the Not Yet
D. The Crucified King
E. The Risen Lord

V. The Last Times (The Descent of the Holy Spirit)

Acts 2:16-18 (ESV) – But this is what was uttered through the prophet Joel: "'And in the last days it shall be,' God declares, 'that I will pour out my Spirit on all flesh, and your sons and your daughters shall prophesy, and your young men shall see visions, and your old men shall dream dreams; even on my male servants and female servants in those days I will pour out my Spirit, and they shall prophesy.'"

A. Between the Times: the Church as
   Foretaste of the Kingdom
B. The Church as Agent of the Kingdom
C. The Conflict Between the Kingdoms
   of Darkness and Light

VI. The Fulfillment of Time (The Second Coming)

Matt. 13:40-43 (ESV) – Just as the weeds are gathered and burned with fire, so will it be at the close of the age. The Son of Man will send his angels, and they will gather out of his Kingdom all causes of sin and all lawbreakers, and throw them into the fiery furnace. In that place there will be weeping and gnashing of teeth. Then the righteous will shine like the sun in the Kingdom of their Father. He who has ears, let him hear.

A. The Return of Christ
B. Judgment
C. The Consummation of His Kingdom

VII. Beyond Time (Eternity Future)

1 Cor. 15:24-28 (ESV) – Then comes the end, when he delivers the Kingdom to God the Father after destroying every rule and every authority and power. For he must reign until he has put all his enemies under his feet. The last enemy to be destroyed is death. For "God has put all things in subjection under his feet." But when it says, "all things are put in subjection," it is plain that he is excepted who put all things in subjection under him. When all things are subjected to him, then the Son himself will also be subjected to him who put all things in subjection under him, that God may be all in all.

A. Kingdom Handed Over to God the Father

B. God as All in All

About the Sacred Roots Project

The Sacred Roots Thriving in Ministry Project seeks to equip and empower under-resourced congregational leaders in urban, rural, and incarcerated communities. One avenue for accomplishing this goal is the Sacred Roots Spiritual Classics, a series of abridged Christian spiritual classics that equip congregational leaders to engage the wealth of the Great Tradition.

Other Sacred Roots Spiritual Classics include:

> *Praying the Psalms with Augustine and Friends*
> Edited by Dr. Carmen Joy Imes
>
> *Becoming a Community of Disciples:*
> *Guildelines from Abbot Benedict and Bishop Basil*
> Edited by Rev. Dr. Greg Peters
>
> *Christian Mission and Poverty:*
> *Wisdom from 2,000 Years of Church Leaders*
> Edited by Rev. Dr. Andrew T. Draper
>
> *Books Jesus Read: Learning from the Apocrypha*
> Edited by Dr. Robert F. Lay
>
> *Renewal in Christ: Athanasius on the Christian Life*
> Edited by Rev. Dr. Jeremy Treat
>
> *Practices of the Ancient Church*
> Edited by Dr. Michael Cooper

Social Justice and Scripture:
Las Casas on Faithful Witness
    Edited by Rev. Dr. Robert Chao Romero
    and Rev. Marcos Canales

Reading the Bible Spiritually
    Edited by Rev. Dr. Greg Peters

Business as Mission: The Journal of John Woolman
    Edited by Dr. Evan B. Howard

Reading the Bible to Meet Jesus
    Edited by Dr. Gregory S. MaGee

Killing Sin:
Lessons on Holiness from John Owens and Phoebe Palmer
    Edited by Dr. Daniel Hill

The Interior Castle
    Edited by Nancy Reyes Frazier

The Autobiography of George Müller
    Edited by Dr. Uche Anizor

The Senior Editorial Team of the Sacred Roots Spiritual Classics includes:

Rev. Dr. Don Davis
Publisher
The Urban Ministry Institute

Rev. Dr. Hank Voss
Executive Editor
Taylor University

Dr. Uche Anizor
Senior Editor
Biola University, Talbot School of Theology

Rev. Dr. Greg Peters
Senior Editor
Biola University, Torrey Honors College

Dr. May Young
Senior Editor
Taylor University

Rev. Ryan Carter
Managing Editor
The Urban Ministry Institute

Isaiah Swain
Managing Editor
Taylor University

The Senior Editorial Team acknowledges and appreciates
Dr. Gwenfair Adams (Gordon-Conwell Theological
Seminary), Dr. Betsy Barber (Biola University), Rev. Dr.
Nigel Black (Winslow Baptist Church), Dr. Jonathan
Calvillo (Boston University School of Divinity), Dr. Laura
Edwards (Taylor University), Rev. Nathan Esla (Lutheran
Bible Translators), Dr. Nancy Frazier (Dallas Theological
Seminary), Dr. Jeff Greenman (Regent College), Dr. Kevin
Hector (University of Chicago Divinity School), Rev. Dr.
Wil Hernandez (Centerquest), Dr. James Houston (Regent
College), Dr. Evan B. Howard (Spirituality Shoppe), Rev.
Susie Krehbiel (Missionary, Retired), Rev. Dr. Tim Larsen
(Wheaton College), Dr. Stephanie Lowery (Africa

International University), Dr. Daniel Owens (Hanoi Bible College), Rev. Dr. Oscar Owens (West Angeles Church of God), Dr. Bob Priest (Taylor University), Rev. Dr. Robert Romero (University of California, Los Angeles), Rev. Dr. Jerry Root (Wheaton College), Dr. Fred Sanders (Biola University), Dr. Glen Scorgie (Bethel University), Dr. Kyle Strobel (Biola University), Dr. Daniel Treier (Wheaton College), and Dr. Kevin Vanhoozer (Trinity Evangelical Divinity School) for their support and encouragement. Illustrations throughout the Sacred Roots Spiritual Classics are done by Naomi Noyes.

The Sacred Roots Spiritual Classics are dedicated to all Christian leaders who have loved the poor and have recognized the importance of Christian spiritual classics for nurturing the next generation. We especially recognize these fourteen:

John Wesley (1703–1791)

Rebecca Protten (1718–1780)

Elizabeth Fry (1780–1845)

Phoebe Palmer (1807–1874)

Dora Yu (1873–1931)

A. W. Tozer (1897–1963)

Howard Thurman (1899–1981)

Watchman Nee (1903–1972)

James Houston (1922–)

J. I. Packer (1926–2020)

Tom Oden (1931–2016)

René Padilla (1932–2021)

Dallas Willard (1935–2013)

Bruce Demarest (1935–2021)

Remember your leaders,
those who spoke to you the word of God.
Consider the outcome of their way of life,
and imitate their faith.

~ Hebrews 13:7

Endnotes

i   Williams' translation updated from "conjugal chastity."

ii   Williams' translation updated from "conjugal chastity," "widow's continence," and "sanctified virginity."

iii   Adapted Williams' translation to follow the translation of Mary Eugenia Laker.

iv   Adapted Williams' translation of the final clause. His original translation read, "he becomes with his friend a single spirit in a single kiss."

v   Williams translates the third kiss as the kiss of "discernment," but I have chosen to translate Aelred's word, *intellectuale*, as "understanding." This "kiss of understanding" or being united with Christ in one Spirit (1 Cor 6:17) was understood by Aelred and his friend Bernard of Clairvaux as abiding continually in Christ (John 15).

vi   In this sentence I have changed *intellectuale* to "understanding" and *gratia* from "favor" to "grace."

vii   "Guts" is in place of "gall."

viii   "Teenagers" for *adolescentium* instead of "young men" and "sexual purity" for *pudicitiam* instead of "chastity."

ix   This sentence is awkward to translate, and I have used Braceland's for the sake of clarity.

x   "Childish" replaces "puerile" as a translation for *puerilis* here and elsewhere.

xi   This sentence modified to follow the translation of Braceland.

xii This sentence has been slightly revised for ease of reading.

xiii This sentence has been slightly revised for ease of reading.

xiv "Talkativeness" replaces "garrulousness."

xv Sentence adapted to follow Laker's translation.

xvi "Praiseworthy" for "probable."

xvii "Fickleness" for "inconstancy."

xviii The Latin word translated as "faithfulness" is *fide*, and it could also be translated "loyalty."

xix "Alter ego" changed to "like another self" following Davidson.

xx "Poor person" for "pauper."

xxi "Correct" for "chastise," here and throughout the text.

xxii Adapted to follow the translation of Braceland.

xxiii Adapted to follow the translation of Braceland.

xxiv "Unbecoming" for "not decorous."

xxv "Respect" substituted for "modesty."

xxvi "Church" for "ecclesiastical."

xxvii "Fawning obedience" for obsequiousness.

Scripture Index

Colossians

1:15, 221
1:16, 221
1:17, 221
1:18, 149
1:28, 82

1 Thessalonians

1:6, 184
2:7, 82
4:16–17, 224
5:14, 151, 154
5:26, 67

1 Timothy

3:15, 222
4:8, 60

2 Timothy

2:8, 222
2:25, 82
4:1, 222

Titus

1:2, 225
2:12, 79, 91

Hebrews

1:3–6, 221
2:10, 221
11, 206
11:35, 207
12:1, 58, 212
13:7, 212, 213, 232
13:12, 221
13:17a, 177

James

1:5, 149
2:25, 207

1 Peter

2:9, 223
2:21, 184
3:21, 222
5:14, 67

2 Peter

1:21, 222

1 John

4:11, 137
4:16, 52
4:18, 162

Revelation

Made in the USA
Middletown, DE
17 June 2023

32311862R00146